Contents

Introduction 2

SEGMENT ONE: OURSELVES
Episode 1   How Do I See Myself? 6
Episode 2   Who Am I Really? 10
Episode 3   Who Can I Become? 14

SEGMENT TWO: OUR GOD
Episode 4   How Do I See God? 18
Episode 5   Is God My Father? 22
Episode 6   What Did Jesus Do for Me? 26
Episode 7   Can God Live in Me? 30
Episode 8   Can God Use Me? 34

SEGMENT THREE: OUR WORLD
Episode 9   What Happens at Home? 38
Episode 10   What Happens at Work? 44
Episode 11   What Happens at Church? 48
Episode 12   What Happens with My Enemies? 54
Episode 13   How Far Does This Go? 58
Feature   *Soul Health* 62
Daily Bible Readings 64

FAITH CAFÉ EDITORS: Kristi Cain, Laura Derico | WRITER: Chris Maxwell | DVD VIDEO PRODUCERS: Charles Powell and Michelle Wheeler

Faith Café is a registered trademark of LifeSprings Resources and is used with permission. Licensed adaptation Copyright © 2007 Standard Publishing. All rights reserved. Published by Standard Publishing, Cincinnati, Ohio. Printed in USA. Scripture, unless otherwise indicated, taken from the HOLY BIBLE, NEW INTERNATIONAL VERSION®. Copyright © 1973, 1978, 1984 International Bible Society. Used by permission of Zondervan. All rights reserved. Scriptures marked *The Message* taken from *The Message*. Copyright © 1993, 1994, 1995, 1996, 2000, 2001, 2002. Used by permission of NavPress Publishing Group. When passages are paraphrased by the editor for the sake of clarity, they are consistent with a commitment to the verbal, plenary inspiration of the Bible. Cover photo © Tim Pannell/Corbis. Interior photos from Dreamstime.com: p. 2 © Zoom-zoom, p. 6 © Ioana Grecu, p. 10 © Luba V Nel, p. 14 © Fabrizio Argonauta, p. 18 © Celso Pupo rodrigues, p. 22 © Henry Fu, p. 26 © Xyno, p. 30 © Stanislav Mikhalev, p. 34 © Wendy Kaveney, p. 38 © Stanislav Mikhalev, p. 44 © Alexey Averiyanov, p. 48 © Elena Kouptsova-vasic, p. 54 © Emin Ozkan, p. 58 © H3ct02, p. 62 © Starfotograf, p. 64 © Boguslaw Kupisinski; from BigStockPhoto.com: p. 3 © Dirk Paessler. All Web site addresses were accurate at the time of printing. Any corrections can be sent to Standard Publishing, www.standardpub.com.

Introduction

Peek in the window of your local coffeehouse. A few people sit with friends; others sit alone. Some listen and others laugh. People talk of weather, business, politics, and the friend who didn't make it there. Conversation goes in many directions, as varied and rich as the shades of coffee beans in the jars that line the wall. Customers come to drink coffee, to relax, to get recharged—but mainly they come together for community.

Many of us are ready to sit together and talk about life—real life, not just the weather or the latest sports scores. To offer you an opportunity to join in the discussion and probe deeper, we welcome you to Faith Café. More than a class and more than a sermon, Faith Café is a place for exploring truth and experiencing eternal change.

We start by studying ourselves: not self-help sessions, but investigations of our own self-views. In these first three episodes we ask, "How Do I See Myself?" "Who Am I Really?" and "Who Can I Become?" Probing Genesis and the Psalms, critiquing excuses, and daring ourselves to face our real lives, we offer opportunities to understand what living on this planet is really about.

The next segment of five episodes turns the attention toward the one who made us what we are and can make us more than we thought we could become. Who is that? You guessed it—God. To better understand God, we've allowed biblical texts, common statistics, and personal stories to lead us toward meaningful answers about him. We also pose some questions too many of us think, but refuse to voice: "How Do I See God?" "Is God My Father?" and "Can God Use Me?"

Moving from ourselves to our God leaves us one place to conclude for the final five episodes: Our World. Again, we find answers by identifying the questions: "What Happens at Home?" "What Happens at Work?" "What Happens at Church?" "What Happens with My Enemies?" and "How Far Does This Go?" These final episodes answer in more detail the earlier question about whether God uses us, and the answer is yes!

ENTER

In our gatherings we do not want you just to sit there and listen. Faith Café invites you to enter into an environment where it is safe to ask for and seek answers. Phrases lure your mind toward deeper paths; quotes dare you to stare into your real self; questions give you a chance to talk to yourself and your friends about what is relevant in your lives.

DRINK

This segment highlights portions of Scripture to help you gain a better understanding of truth, while friends beside you voice their own reflections about how the biblical story inspires them to believe in new ways. Your soul can be refreshed by drinking in the living water of God's Word.

SAVOR

You will savor the stories of the struggles, musings, and triumphs of imperfect people like us who are journeying into a deeper relationship with Jesus. You will get a taste of ancient reality as it touches our fast-paced culture. And these bites of life will help to guide, challenge, and focus you.

EXPERIENCE

Faith Café also offers statistics to investigate, books to read, video clips to watch, Web sites to peruse, and thoughts to ponder. The discussions of our society today will provoke groups to enter and experience lessons together. You'll create community and in doing so, learn more about yourself.

WALK

As we examine society's trends and scrutinize Christianity's core beliefs, we choose not to leave it there. We offer suggestions to walk out with the truth you've explored and straightforward strategies for declaring doctrine daily to those around you. Actions such as writing letters, serving meals, or visiting hospitals will allow you to take your faith and share the delight with desperate people.

Every session includes an invitation to experience the truth you're studying on a regular basis. Spiritual disciplines such as intercession, silence, worship, study, and journaling help move you toward transformation. Your heavenly Father can guide and change you as you evaluate your habits and lifestyle.

You are invited to taste and see, to drink and be refreshed. By reflecting and exploring, by examining and investigating, by meditating and applying, you just might discover a way to know God more and to get closer to the person he created you to be. We have no doubt you'll be glad you decided to sit, sip, and talk about life at Faith Café.

A Word for Leaders

Thanks to cell phones and the Internet, communication has never been easier, yet many people suffer from spiritual loneliness. But what if a small group created real community? What if the group's members confessed their worries, hurts, and fears in an environment where hope stays alive? What if friends sat beside friends seeking ways to develop deep, real, alive relationships with their maker? What if people joined together and began a journey of Christian spiritual formation?

Faith Café curriculum was designed for the person seeking this kind of experience. Real growth with real community. Authentic souls seeking to serve others.

Paul encouraged the church at Ephesus saying, "Then we will no longer be infants, tossed back and forth by the waves, and blown here and there by every wind of teaching. . . . Instead, speaking the truth in love, we will in all things grow up into him who is the Head, that is, Christ" (Ephesians 4:14, 15). Just like the Ephesians, we were never meant to receive Christ's salvation and then sit back and do nothing. We were meant to know Jesus and, as a result of getting to know him, to be changed. We believe that Faith Café will help you and your group to grow up in Christ together.

FAITH CAFÉ FEATURES

Faith Café has been designed with leaders in mind. Though we've called this a Leader's Guide, we know that you will want to be a part of this group, not just a face on the other side of a podium. To that end, we provide you with tools to facilitate honest connections and encourage lively, thoughtful discussions. Here's some of what you'll find useful in the five parts that make up each Faith Café episode: ENTER, DRINK, SAVOR, EXPERIENCE, and WALK.

Quotes to think about
Especially in the ENTER section, but also in other parts of each episode, quotes are provided from a variety of writers, performers, and thinkers. In the **Consider it** box, you'll find a quotation that was selected in particular to allow the group to reflect on an aspect of that episode's message or to engage in debate about a meaningful topic.

Scripture support
Though each episode in your leader's guide handily contains all the text that exists in the participant's guide, we've also added some material to be beneficial to you as you walk others through the Bible passages. In Go Deeper, you'll find insightful information that could help answer questions about or provide context for that episode's Scripture. This section may also contain discussion questions to help you and the members of your group flesh out the message in God's Word.

Facilitating ideas
Besides the Scripture supporting information, each episode is packed with illustrations, activities, media elements, and discussion options that will help to engage every sort of learning style. A **Look into it** box offers

Web sites, books, and other suggestions for further research. And there are no rigid rules or regulations in Faith Café: you may feel free to pick and choose from among the offerings, use none, or use them all!

Adaptable design
We've provided you with some fuel and flavor, but the particular experience is yours to create. Faith Café curriculum is written in a way that allows you to adapt the episode to your own group's unique tastes. Maybe you'll want to start with a bite of life from the SAVOR section one week, and end with a refreshing DRINK from the living Word the next. Or maybe you'll want to follow the order on the page. You and your group can decide what best suits your appetite.

Strategies for service
We don't want your Faith Café experience to end inside the walls of your meeting room. We provide you with simple actions and strategies for taking what you've learned to go—hoping you will make a difference in your community each week and by doing so, stretch and grow in your faith. Spiritual disciplines are also suggested, offering each group member yet another way to care for their souls throughout the week.

SETTING THE SCENE

You may be wondering, *OK, I've got the tools, now where do I start?* We believe that creating a certain kind of environment is an important part of this experience. Think about your favorite coffeehouse or café. What descriptive words do you think of? *Inviting. Relaxing. Warm.* Now imagine how you could recreate that setting for your group. It may be as simple as bringing in a couple of lamps for softer lighting, or arranging the seats in a circle so everyone can see each other. What resources does your group have available? Maybe you can find comfortable chairs and cozy couches at your local thrift store. Will you have a large group? Maybe you can use a tall stool to speak from instead of standing. Make it a multi-sensory experience. Have music playing as group members arrive. Don't forget the necessary equipment for playing the Faith Café DVD clips! And finally, think about bringing snacks, drinks, and of course, coffee, to complete the scene. See www.standardpub.com/faithcafe for more ideas on creating a Faith Café space in your church.

It's important to remember that community will happen only in a trusting and authentic atmosphere. This may take a few weeks to cultivate, but know that people are hungry for a place where they can truly be known and know others. Be willing to share your own struggles, doubts, or dreams to demonstrate the importance of honest dialogue. Be sensitive to the questions or pains that others share by taking time to talk through issues and pray, even if it means leaving out a portion of the lesson. Be patient with those who are quiet or shy by giving them time to get comfortable in this new environment.

Finally, pray. Pray that God will bring about dramatic transformation. Pray that he will build relationships that go deep and stand strong. As you can see, Faith Café is more than a topical curriculum that happens once a week. It's a place to create a community that can change lives. If you're interested in designing such a space in your church, Faith Café is for you. You're invited to taste and see, to drink and be refreshed. Come on in—everyone is welcome.

EPISODE 1 | OURSELVES

How Do I See Myself?

SUPPLIES NEEDED
Paper and pens or pencils
Faith Café DVD

ENTER

Are you feeling as if God is way off in the distance? Or maybe you're not sure where you are in your relationship with him?

Welcome God to the "café" of your inner life . . . that place where the real *you* lives, where the creature God made lives, where hurts and hopes and anger and joy all merge.

Offer this request: *God, as I seek to learn more about myself and about you, I ask you to forgive me of my mistakes and welcome me into your café. Thanks.*

These café conversations are about living life—about not just believing that a real spiritual experience is possible, but helping it happen. Enter the café and relax, breathe, look around. You never know what you'll find there. Today you might find you.

As the leader, begin each lesson in prayer. Offer a gentle, nonthreatening chance for participants to voice their own prayers silently. Anyone who isn't a follower of Christ can be guided in a prayer of welcome (see the prayer above) that he or she can silently pray along with you.

Offer a sheet of paper and pen or pencil to each participant. Then read the text below. Remind the class that when an order is placed at this spiritual café, it is really a request, not a demand. But God longs to hear our inner desires. After a few minutes, let them hide their orders. Then move to the next part.

It's time to place an order at the Faith Café. Order your inner desires. No one is going to see this except you and God. As you think through the menu in your mind, ask yourself these questions:

- What do I hide about myself?
- What words would describe how I see myself and my relationship with God right now?
- Who do I wish I could become?
- What words do I wish described me?
- Is that order, or request, possible in my life right now? If not, why not? If so, how?

Consider it
"They cannot parody you unless they know you, and when they know you, it means you're part of the culture, and when you're part of the culture, it means you're successful."
—Joan Rivers, from an interview in *The Week*

Read the quote above and have a quick-hit conversation about what it means. If you have time, break your group into two sections and let them debate the truth or falsehood of the statement. Who thinks Joan Rivers's comment about being a success is right? Who doesn't? Give each group just one minute to come up with their argument and one minute to present it to the other side. End the time by asking the whole group to keep their thoughts about success and failure in mind as you read the Scripture together.

DRINK

Read aloud the passage from Lamentations. Read slowly and with a serious tone.

> Oh, oh, oh . . . How empty the city,
> once teeming with people.
> A widow, this city,
> once in the front rank of nations,
> once queen of the ball,
> she's now a drudge in the kitchen.
> She cries herself to sleep each night,
> tears soaking her pillow.
> No one's left among her lovers to sit and
> hold her hand.
> Her friends have all dumped her.
> —Lamentations 1:1, 2 (*The Message*)

Lamentations is a book in the Bible that depicts the Jewish nation as a widow—a sad, lonely, defeated widow. Formerly ranked at the top, the nation had fallen to the bottom. Think of hurricanes or fires ruining neighborhoods and cities. Think of terrorist attacks changing a world. The Israelites must have felt destroyed, defeated, unwelcome anywhere and by anyone. They wondered if even God wanted them anymore.

Do you ever feel as if you are at the bottom? History helps us remember that Israel did not have to remain there. They were God's chosen people—set apart by God to be his own. To be loved.

As you trek through your own journey, you can join Israel in noticing what you think of yourself and what you should do to move forward. And you can remember that you don't have to stay where you are. You too are God's own. You are loved by God.

GO DEEPER

Follow up the Scripture reading with a few reminders about what was going on at that time in Israel. Keep the flow personal and not academic. Let the listeners do more that realize history; help them relate to it.

Probably written by Jeremiah, the book of Lamentations is a painful confession of sadness. The nation of Israel felt defeated. Jerusalem had been destroyed by the Chaldeans (the historical Babylonians, sixth century BC). Enemies had overrun their holy places, tearing down their temple, imprisoning their king, and enslaving their people. They were asking God questions about why everything had happened and how they could get out of this disaster. You can see why this collection of poetic prayers, Lamentations, was originally called by a Hebrew word which means "How?" Its purpose was to offer a song of wailing.

Feelings of sadness like that flow through our inner thoughts but don't hit the song list of our praise and worship services. The Israelites would read this book aloud to remind themselves about a city's falling, about sin, and about sadness. Rather than denying pain and rejection, they prayed it out corporately and regularly.

Ask the group these questions:

- How would you have felt if you were Jeremiah, writing about your nation being destroyed?
- What do you think was going on inside Jeremiah?
- The nation of Israel viewed herself as damaged villages. How might our own lives be considered damaged villages? How could confessing these verses help us to let go of our hurt?
- How many people do you know who pray just like this Scripture, feeling empty and alone as they cry themselves to sleep every night? How have you been able to reach out to someone like that? What was the response?
- When do you feel lonely or empty? What do you do about it?

SAVOR

Have a member or members of the group read this section aloud.

Betty listened. She appreciated the speaker's honesty about the value of relationships. At one point, her mind wandered. His words about loving others lured her thoughts in a new direction. She questioned whether she had ever really loved anyone. Betty remembered the facial expression of a friend and asked herself, *What did I do to make her so angry?* She recalled the departure of a spouse and said, *Why did I blow it?* She realized that she isn't very close to many people and thought, *I can't blame them; I wouldn't be around myself if I didn't have to.*

Compare Betty's thoughts with these: "I'm so grateful to Christ Jesus for making me adequate to do this work. . . . The only credentials I brought to it were invective and witch hunts and arrogance. But I was treated mercifully because I didn't know what I was doing—didn't know who I was doing it against! Grace mixed with faith and love poured over me and into me. And all because of Jesus. Here's a word you can take to heart and depend on: Jesus Christ came into the world to save sinners. I'm proof—Public Sinner Number One—of someone who could never have made it apart from sheer mercy" (1 Timothy 1:12-19, *The Message*).

Involve the class in discussion.

1. Voice one word that describes Betty. (For example, blaming, self-hating, condemned, guilty, lies, faults, disapproving, critical, isolated.) Was there ever a time that word could have been used to describe you? When was that?

2. Why do so many of us think the way Betty thinks?

3. Compare Betty's words and attitude with those of Paul, as seen in the letter to Timothy. How are they similar? How are they different?

4. Do you think it is OK for followers of Christ to be sad and express their sorrow? Why or why not?

5. Why do we feel pressure to appear happy and unblemished all the time?

6. What are some healthy ways we can admit our sadness and our failures? How could being honest with ourselves about our sin be helpful to us? to others?

EXPERIENCE

Read or let someone read the paragraph below. Then ask the questions that follow.

Comedian Joan Rivers has had bags removed from under her eyes, two complete face-lifts, cheek implants, fat injections, brow smoothing, teeth capping, neck tightening, a tummy tuck, and a nose thinning. She is quoted as saying, "When you look better, you are treated differently. People want to be around attractive people" (from "The New and Improved Rivers," *The Week*, July 15, 2005).

Does changing your outward appearance ever make you feel better inside? Why or why not? What does the approval of others mean to you?

Thoughts to share: Watching how others view us can influence who we think we are and prompt us to find ways to change ourselves. Depending on the opinion of others can damage our view of ourselves.

Seeking applause by performing or pretending doesn't help us in changing who we really are. Nor does it truly bring success. Even the approval of others doesn't make us really better people. We are much better in life when we seek God's approval, when we accept his acceptance. Insecurity can turn into true security, even without a joke or a face-lift.

Look into it
- Psalm 8
- David Gregory, *Dinner With a Perfect Stranger: An Invitation Worth Considering*
- www.dinnerwithaperfectstranger.com

WALK

Do you want to move from sadness in yourself to acceptance of yourself? Do you want to stop lamenting and start rejoicing? Then realize God's love. This doesn't mean that you have to just sweep away your doubts or your negative self-talk. Admit and confess your inner struggle. But be willing to "take out" the truth you've learned today. As you might say in a real café, "I'll get this to go!"

Read or have someone read this quote:

"God loves you so much he wants what is best for you. He also wants to know if you want what is best for yourself."
— Stephen Arterburn, *Healing Is a Choice*

Ask these questions: What does Arterburn's comment say to you? What do you think he means?

Play the Episode 1 clip from the Faith Café DVD.
Ask these questions: Does God really love us? How can we be changed if we know this? How can we choose to know about God's love? How can we tell others that God really likes them?

Read the "to go" assignments to the class, or ask them to read them, and encourage them to make a commitment to do at least one of the actions and to practice the spiritual discipline.

Carry a mug of God's love with you as you go through your week:

- E-mail someone who feels alone. Serve that person the meal of encouragement.
- Call someone you know isn't home. Leave a short message on the answering machine and try to encourage that person with your words and tone so he or she feels accepted.
- Look at yourself in the mirror. Tell yourself God loves you. Repeat the phrase seven times.

This week's spiritual discipline is journaling: Write about any obstacle that is currently dragging you down or maybe hurting your relationship with God. Write your own lament. Then think about who you want to become and who God has created you to become. Write about it.

End your class together by suggesting that each person read Psalm 8 every day for a week. This can help prepare their minds for the next phase. You may want to read it aloud to them.

O Lord, our Lord,
how majestic is your name in all the earth!
You have set your glory
above the heavens.
From the lips of children and infants
you have ordained praise
because of your enemies,
to silence the foe and the avenger.
When I consider your heavens,
the work of your fingers,
the moon and the stars,
which you have set in place,
what is man that you are mindful of him,
the son of man that you care for him?
You made him a little lower than the heavenly beings
and crowned him with glory and honor.
You made him ruler over the works of your hands;
you put everything under his feet:
all flocks and herds,
and the beasts of the field,
the birds of the air,
and the fish of the sea,
all that swim the paths of the seas.
O Lord, our Lord,
how majestic is your name in all the earth!

NOTES

EPISODE 2 | OURSELVES

Who Am I Really?

SUPPLIES NEEDED
Mirror
Faith Café DVD

ENTER

"I am afraid to show you who I really am, you might not like it—and that's all I got."
—Sabrina Ward Harrison

In the last episode we talked about our self-views. Understanding how we see ourselves is crucial to becoming even better than we are. It's like making sure we know where we are on the map before taking the next turn. Today we continue the journey of investigating our lives as we digest the amazing taste of the truth. But before your next sip of coffee, ask yourself, "What do I really think about myself? How does that compare to what God thinks?"

Begin moving toward an opportunity to change who you think you are, and then change who you hope to become.

"Whose approval do you crave? Have there been times when you have sought the applause of men over the approval of God? How did you feel afterwards?"
—Mark Atteberry, *The Climb of Your Life*

Ask those joining you to talk about any questions or revelations that may have come up through their practice of journaling last week. See if anyone has an experience of serving others to share. Give them a moment to invite God here through silent prayer.

After a brief time of silence, bring out a mirror and pass it around. The mirror should be small enough to pass around but large enough for people to see themselves. Read the questions in the box below, allowing time for people to answer them inwardly or, if they are comfortable doing so, reveal their answers to the group.

> Take a moment to look in a mirror. As you look at yourself from various angles, think about these questions:
> - What do you like about what you see?
> - What do you not like?
> - How would you describe the person in the mirror to others?
> - How much do you think your outer image resembles the person you are on the inside?

Talk about how we all reach certain conclusions when we look in a mirror. Our views of ourselves shape how we make decisions, how we place blame, how we take responsibility, and how we deal with emotions.

Consider it
"Fact: It takes about twenty positive statements about ourselves . . . to counteract just one negative personal statement!"
—Heidi J. Raynor, ed. by Dr. C. River Smith, "Negative Self-Talk and Your Self-Esteem"

Direct the group's attention to the Consider it *quote and ask for a show of hands as to how many people agree with the fact presented there. If time allows, encourage people to share any experiences they have had that reflect the truth of that quote.*

DRINK

Read this text out loud. Remember to read it with a tone of voice that lets everyone know you are reading a wonderful story!

God said, "Let us make man in our image, in our likeness, and let them rule over the fish of the sea and the birds of the air, over the livestock, over all the earth, and over all the creatures that move along the ground."

So God created man in his own image, in the image of God he created him; male and female he created them.

God blessed them and said to them, "Be fruitful and increase in number; fill the earth and subdue it. Rule over the fish of the sea and the birds of the air and over every living creature that moves on the ground."

Then God said, "I give you every seed-bearing plant on the face of the whole earth and every tree that has fruit with seed in it. They will be yours for food. And to all the beasts of the earth and all the birds of the air and all the creatures that move on the ground—everything that has the breath of life in it—I give every green plant for food." And it was so.

God saw all that he had made, and it was very good. And there was evening, and there was morning—the sixth day.

—Genesis 1:26-31

GO DEEPER

Understanding the first design of human life is vital to guiding our thoughts about ourselves. No matter what others think about us, or what we assume they think about us, can't we believe what the book of Genesis says? Look again to those verses and read these statements to your group:

- "So God created man in his own image."
- "In the image of God he created him."
- "Male and female he created them."

Remind everyone of the conclusion God reached as he observed what he had made:

- "God saw all that he had made, and it was very good."

Voice together this version of those statements:

- So God created *me* in his own image!
- In the image of God I was created!
- All men and women are made by God in his image!
- God sees all that he has made, and smiles!
- God says, "I love what I see!"

SAVOR

The man told Chuck, "You look just like your mama." Chuck smiled, nodding in kindness to a distant relative he hadn't seen in years. He laughed inside because a few minutes before, another person had said, "I feel like I'm looking at your dad whenever I see you."

Chuck had heard it all before: whom he looks like, talks like, and acts like. Instead of being bothered by the comparisons, Chuck chose to do his own self-evaluation. He grabbed his Palm device and wrote these questions before any more aunts or uncles could offer their critiques:

1. What do people think when they see me?
2. What do I think about myself?
3. Who am I really?
4. How does God view me?
5. How can I truly believe I'm made in the image of God?'

Pose Chuck's questions to the members of your group. Give them a few moments to think, and then allow some to voice brief answers.

EXPERIENCE

Play Episode 2 clip from the Faith Café DVD.

Engage the group in a short discussion using questions such as these: What has made the biggest impression on you so far today? What are you thinking about right now, considering all we've discussed and heard?

After the video clip, invite the group to discuss the article on self-talk (below). You can just give a summary of the article, or someone could read it aloud. Do they agree with what's being said there, or not? How would anyone go about replacing negative self-talk with positive self-talk?

Q: What is self-esteem?

A: Self-esteem is our internal feelings and evaluation of ourselves based on our perceived self-image.

Self-esteem and self-image are closely interrelated and are largely based on our feedback while growing up ([from] parents, peers, other important figures).

Fact: It takes about twenty positive statements about ourselves (the foundation of our self-image/self-esteem) to counteract just one negative personal statement!

Here's the difficult part: It doesn't take a continual repetition of negative statements from our parents, peers, and others throughout our childhood to cause low self-image/self-esteem. . . . Once we get a couple in our head, we can use them over and over again. Again and again, we take those false negatives and repeat them unconsciously (completely unaware). It's like having a constant heckler with you.

Can counseling help? Most definitely. . . . We need to replace negative self-talk with positive self-talk that we're willing to let ourselves accept. You can't draw on a chalkboard if there's an eraser following close behind. [Negative self-talk] erases the good, and replenishes it with bad.

—from Heidi J. Raynor, ed. by Dr. C. River Smith, "Negative Self-Talk and Your Self-Esteem"

(© 1998 allaboutcounseling.com)

Look into it
- Psalm 139
- Timothy Jones, *Awake My Soul: Practical Spirituality for Busy People*
- Dr. Larry Crabb, *Understanding People*

WALK

What did you learn from the mirror? from the story of how God created us? from Chuck's story? from Larry Crabb (in the video clip)? from the article on negative self-talk and self-esteem?

Let what you learned strengthen you to work and serve throughout your week. If you are a little timid about reaching out, read this:

"If you wait until you're really sure, you'll never take off the training wheels."

—Cynthia Copeland Lewis

Look into a mirror again. Choose to view yourself in a new way. Let today's truth change how you see that reflection—that handsome/beautiful, created-in-God's-image you!

- Think of a person toward whom you feel a little jealousy. Pray for him or her every day this week. Pray blessings, peace, and joy for that person, who is made in the image of God.
- Visit a local hospital, retirement center, or elderly persons' housing development. Remind those you see how God sees them.

This week's spiritual discipline is silence: Take time to be still, to think, and to hear the sound of silence. Work through the discomfort and find comfort with yourself.

Talk with the group about which parts of today's session stood out for them. Pass the mirror around again and read the text in the box above. Admit to the group that not one of us is ever totally ready to do what he or she is created to do. But, rather than waiting, we all can give today's nourishment to others in simple ways.

Encourage the group to practice the discipline of silence. Give them a few moments to try it now. After a few minutes, close your time together in prayer, asking God to reveal his truth to the group throughout the week. Read the Scripture below.

"I thank my God every time I remember you. In all my prayers for all of you, I always pray with joy because of your partnership in the gospel from the first day until now, being confident of this, that he who began a good work in you will carry it on to completion until the day of Christ Jesus."

—Philippians 1:3-6

NOTES

EPISODE 3 | OURSELVES

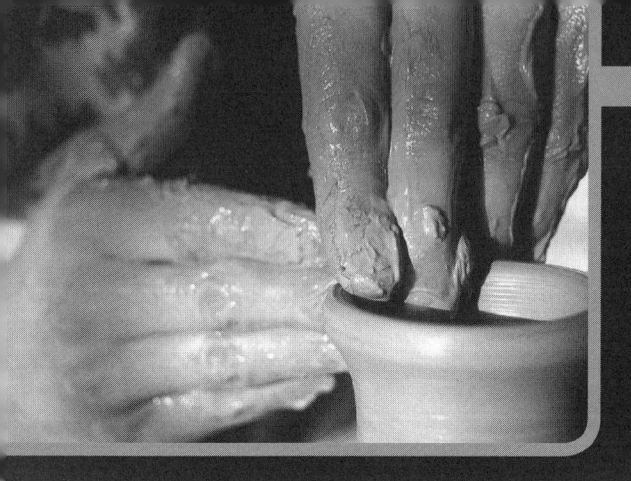

Who Can I Become?

SUPPLIES NEEDED

"Who Am I?" by Casting Crowns, from the album *Casting Crowns*

Poster board and marker, white board and marker, or chalkboard and chalk

Mirror

Picture of Jesus to attach to the mirror

Tape

ENTER

If we believe God made us, why do we let so much other junk invade our thoughts and feelings? Why can't we focus on the honor and privilege of being made by the all-knowing God? He made us. He really made us. And he is still at work in our lives, reshaping us with his care.

Take some time to reflect on these thoughts.

"We cannot become what we need to be by remaining what we are."

—Max De Pree

"Everybody thinks of changing humanity, and nobody thinks of changing himself."

—Leo Tolstoy

After people have had time to settle into their seats, read the two above quotes out loud, and begin the class with prayer. Then read the text from the box below. Have the group reread the four bulleted points with you. They don't need to answer, but you may want to pose this question: Do you believe these things about yourself today?

> The way we hope to "become what we need to be" and change humanity by changing ourselves depends on believing these facts:
> - I was made in the image of God.
> - I have spiritual gifts.
> - I am called for such a time as this.
> - I am influencing the world.

Consider it

"Being able to label your gift(s) is not of utmost importance. Using your gift(s) is."

—from the Ministry Tools Resource Center, http://MinTools.com

Have some discussion about the Consider it quote. Do people agree or disagree? Use this time to bring up questions or frustrations people may have about the topic of spiritual gifts. Encourage people to be honest about their feelings or opinions. Tell the group: Today we may not find all the answers, but we'll look at ways to get there and talk about how not to get stuck in the confusion.

DRINK

Read or have someone read the verses below.

Oh yes, you shaped me first inside, then out;
you formed me in my mother's womb.
I thank you, High God—you're breathtaking!

14 | FAITH CAFÉ

Body and soul, I am marvelously made!
I worship in adoration—what a creation!
You know me inside and out,
you know every bone in my body;
You know exactly how I was made, bit by bit,
how I was sculpted from nothing into something.
Like an open book, you watched me grow from conception to birth;
all the stages of my life were spread out before you,
The days of my life all prepared
before I'd even lived one day.
—Psalm 139:13-16 (*The Message*)

Lead the group to think about what David wrote in that Psalm. God—who created the universe and everything in it—shaped you, inside and out. God formed you. Isn't that an honor? Let us choose to be honored by those beliefs.

Read verse 14 aloud again:
I thank you, High God—you're breathtaking!
Body and soul, I am marvelously made!
I worship in adoration—what a creation!

GO DEEPER

David's honest confession from Psalm 139 was a poetic prayer reminding himself and his nation of their true purpose.

David stated intimate beliefs. Doctrine about God became clear as David sang out his beliefs. In presenting the omniscience of God—the all-knowing, aware-of-everything, never-surprised God—David used creative phrases and not defensive arguments.

The God who searches, hears, sees, creates, knows, and loves is the true God who has put in place the real meaning of life. The omniscient God is also the loving and accepting God.

"God's character goes into the creation of every person. When you feel worthless or even begin to hate yourself, remember that God's Spirit is ready and willing to work within you. We should have as much respect for ourselves as our Maker has for us."
—Life Application Notes

Though it is wonderful to know that God knows us "inside and out" and yet still loves us, this knowledge can also be challenging. At the end of Psalm 139, David asks God to search him, test him, and see if he has done anything wrong. How many of us honestly invite God to do that? Yet if we want to grow and become who God created us to be, we need to do just that. We need to confess our mistakes, admit our faults, and give God a real chance to change us.

SAVOR

Have several members of the group take turns reading paragraphs of the story.

Do we really want to recognize our strengths and build on them while admitting our weaknesses and finding help? Moving forward, instead of moving out, works.

I asked a friend how he moved forward, learning to walk again after a car accident. He said, "I worked and refused to stop until I walked. Then every morning I would wake up and have to force myself to walk again."

I asked a lady who had battled an eating disorder since her teen years how she moved forward. She said, "I focused on my positives and worked to improve them. I also confessed my weaknesses with total honesty and asked others to help me. If my friends had never confronted me to find help, I might not have changed."

I asked an alcoholic how he faced his addiction and won the battle. He said, "I had to admit what I was really like. For too long I claimed not to have any problems. It helped me when I finally got help. Three times a day I voice my vows and pleas to God in prayer. Now, four years and seven months since my last drink, I keep moving forward one step at a time."

I asked a lady if she still struggles to forgive her

husband for his affair. She said, "Remember when you told me to walk through the house and read the Scriptures loudly? Things have been better since then. I know it was more than that. The counseling, the prayers, the forgiveness, and knowing he is now held accountable. But it is like something happened in the house, or maybe in my spirit, that gave me hope again. I keep hearing you say that I need to remember how God also has forgiven me. Looking back, I'm so glad I didn't just run from the situation—or murder him—like I wanted to."

I asked a friend in prison what she would say to those of us who are still living in freedom. She said, "Stop wasting time. Don't make stupid decisions. Trust me, you don't want to end up here. But I also worry about those people who keep doing things that will never get them into prison. Their habits keep them locked in a different kind of prison. I'll tell you this, I am more free here—even though I hate it—than I was living that life of drugs."

Before I ended my visit in the federal prison, I asked the young lady to pray for me. Her honesty took reverence to another level. She didn't play a game. She pleaded to a listening Rescuer. Her prayer motivated me to stop wasting time.

(from Chris Maxwell, *Changing My Mind: A Journey of Disability and Joy*)

EXPERIENCE

Discuss the questions below with the group.

Think of this quote from *Changing My Mind*: "Moving forward, instead of moving out, works." Why do so many of us choose to "move out," to escape or avoid who we are and doubt who we can ever become? Wouldn't we be better off "moving forward"—finding our true selves and stepping toward accomplishment? What could make that more likely for you?

Encourage those who are interested to take one of the personality profiles or spiritual gifts tests listed in Look into it. *Remind participants to ask friends outside this group what they think their spiritual gifts and natural talents might be. By knowing ourselves better, we can work toward fulfilling our dreams and trusting God's guidance. Offer these suggestions:*

- *Ask your friends to tell you what they see in you.*
- *Make a list of positives in your life.*
- *Thank your creator.*
- *Choose to use the gifts God has given you.*
- *Look in the mirror and smile at yourself!*

Say: We are often afraid to admit our talents, so let's talk about them, but give God the credit! What can you do through gifts and talents for the work of God? What has held you back from using those talents?

Look into it
- www.christianet.com/bible/spiritualgiftstest.htm
- www.christianet.com/bible/personalitytests.htm
- www.mintools.com/gifts3.htm
- www.mintools.com/spiritual-gifts-test.htm
- www.advisorteam.org/the_four-temperaments
- www.keirsey.com/matrix.html
- www.personalitypage.com/four-temps.html
- Stephen Arterburn, *Healing Is a Choice*

Consider playing the song "Who Am I?" by Casting Crowns. After it ends, have the group read portions of the song in random order. Encourage each member of the class to read the Scriptures (Psalms 52 and 139 and Ephesians 2) referenced in the lyrics.

Who Am I?
Who am I, that the Lord of all the earth
Would care to know my name,
Would care to feel my hurt?
Who am I, that the Bright and Morning Star
Would choose to light the way
For my ever wandering heart?
Not because of who I am,
But because of what You've done,
Not because of what I've done
But because of who You are.

Chorus:
I am a flower quickly fading,
Here today and gone tomorrow,
A wave tossed in the ocean,
A vapor in the wind.
Still You hear me when I'm calling;
Lord, You catch me when I'm falling,
And You've told me who I am:
I am Yours, I am Yours.
Who am I, that the eyes that see my sin
Would look on me with love and watch me rise again?
Who Am I, that the voice that calmed the sea
Would call out through the rain
And calm the storm in me?
I am Yours;
Whom shall I fear?
Whom shall I fear
'Cause I am Yours;
I am Yours.

Written by Mark Hall. Music by Casting Crowns. © 2003 Club Zoo Music / SWECS Music (Admin. by Club Zoo Music) / BMI. All rights reserved. Used by permission.

WALK

Put this quote on a poster, white board or chalkboard. Have the class read it together.

"Reduce the human job description down to one phrase, and this is it: Reflect God's glory."
—Max Lucado, *It's Not About Me*

If you think about that job description, how are we doing? What is our potential? How can we reach it?

Put a picture or other reminder of Jesus near your mirror. Realize that you are created to represent him. That is not adding pressure to condemn you. Rather than living under judgment, we can accept this realization as an honor and live it out in the hurried tasks of everyday life. Let's do it!

Place a picture of Jesus on a mirror. Tell the class it's time again to look in the mirror. Encourage them to think about the phrase reflect God's glory. *Emphasize how Christ is now showing his love through his followers. As people see us, they have a chance to see his love.*

Take today's lesson to someone.
"I'm telling the solemn truth: Whenever you did one of these things to someone overlooked or ignored, that was me—you did it to me."
—Matthew 25:40 (*The Message*)

This week's spiritual discipline is solitude:
To be in solitude means to hide away, to be alone, to reflect calmly upon ourselves and our lives. Take time to exit your normal rush, your common crowded and covered world. Rather than hiding away to escape problems, we can hide away with God, giving him our time. The private silence and stillness alone with God allow us to observe him and remember how he observes us—his creation. Enter the world of solitude and truly believe you are wonderfully made by God.

Ask: Now that you know who you are, how can you take God's image to those who are sad and lonely so they can see it? Is there someone in your life who could benefit from something you learned today? If so, how might you share that message of truth this week?

Take a few moments to pray for the people sitting closest to you. Ask God to help them be more aware of how they reflect his image. Pray each one will have the courage to act out what has been discussed.

NOTES

EPISODE 4 | OUR GOD

How Do I See God?

SUPPLIES NEEDED
Movie clip: *Bruce Almighty* (19:20–23:15)
Faith Café DVD

ENTER

These studies and discussions are about much more than believing in an Almighty God. They are about a relationship with a God we believe in. So let's investigate our present thoughts, views, and feelings about God and begin a journey with him that we have never had before. What might happen? A door may be unlocked; pain may be healed; dirt may be washed away; a world may be changed.

To move forward, it is best to know where we already are. We sometimes get glimpses of the state of our faith in unexpected places, such as while we're on a trip or when we're working on our finances. Understanding our spiritual condition can help us grow. In order to improve our relationship with God, we must also sometimes critique and confess our present view of God.

We have spent a few weeks finding out more about ourselves, but is that where we stop? Is that all there is?

Pray: *God, as we pursue a better knowledge of you and a relationship with you, help us grasp how we view you now. Lure us away from what is wrong, and dare us to dive into the truth of who you are.*

Pray the above prayer with the group. Then read the following quote from Ecclesiastes. Acknowledge that even writers of the Bible felt confusion and frustration in trying to know God. Discuss the questions in the box that follow.

"True, God made everything beautiful in itself and in its time—but he's left us in the dark, so we can never know what God is up to, whether he's coming or going.
—Ecclesiastes 3:11 (*The Message*)

A relationship with God.
- How do you feel when you hear those words?
- What thoughts or images come to your mind?
- What memories and fears invade as you think of having a true relationship with God?

Consider it
"When Christians say that they have faith in God, what do they mean? Do they know what they mean? Do they even mean anything at all?
—Austin Cline, "Faith in God, Faith in Mumbo Jumbo" (http://atheism.about.com)

If time allows, discuss the Consider it *quote. Ask:*
- *How much do you think the way believers talk about their faith affects how nonbelievers see God?*
- *How might having an unclear picture of what your faith in God means hurt your ability to tell others about him?*
- *Do you know what you mean when you say you have faith in God?*

18 | FAITH CAFÉ

DRINK

Have several participants share the reading.

Surely, O God, you have worn me out;
you have devastated my entire household.
You have bound me—and it has become a witness;
my gauntness rises up and testifies against me.
God assails me and tears me in his anger
and gnashes his teeth at me;
my opponent fastens on me his piercing eyes.
Men open their mouths to jeer at me;
they strike my cheek in scorn
and unite together against me.
God has turned me over to evil men
and thrown me into the clutches of the wicked.
All was well with me, but he shattered me;
he seized me by the neck and crushed me.
He has made me his target;
his archers surround me.
Without pity, he pierces my kidneys
and spills my gall on the ground.
Again and again he bursts upon me;
he rushes at me like a warrior.
I have sewed sackcloth over my skin
and buried my brow in the dust.
My face is red with weeping,
deep shadows ring my eyes;
yet my hands have been free of violence
and my prayer is pure.
O earth, do not cover my blood;
may my cry never be laid to rest!
Even now my witness is in heaven;
my advocate is on high.
My intercessor is my friend
as my eyes pour out tears to God;
on behalf of a man he pleads with God
as a man pleads for his friend.

—Job 16:7-21

GO DEEPER

The book of Job is like nothing else in the Bible. A man who had so much lost it all. He stayed alive, but he lived a much different life. Think about it: losing wealth and family and reputation; having friends add more problems as they try to help. Job had so much but lost it all.

Well, he didn't actually lose it all. He still had God. And he decided to be totally honest with the God he served. The dialogue between Job and God and between Job and his so-called friends fills the pages of this book, written by an unknown author at an unspecified time.

Although Job wondered what had really happened, God had not abandoned him. The God who knew Job loved Job. The wealthy landowner and livestock owner, whose name means "he that weeps," lost all but what mattered most: God.

What can we learn from this story? Then, as now, people would often see having health and wealth as a sign of God's favor. As people turn toward God asking for a sudden shift toward pleasure, maybe Job's sad experience can keep our focus correct. God doesn't always fix things our way at our time.

Just see how it all ends. The God Job trusted stayed true. Though pain and problems did not stay away, Job stayed true. His questions, doubts, anger, and uncertainty led him deeper into the God-guided life, not further away.

Remind the group that each of us can learn from Job's pain. We can learn from his response. We can choose to go deeper with God even during life's storms.

Ask: What does God want to teach us today through this story? How can we apply it in our normal lives? What can we do to help others who are angry with God, instead of responding as Job's friends responded?

Read this psalm to the group. Then discuss the questions that follow.

Lord, you have been our dwelling place
throughout all generations.
Before the mountains were born
or you brought forth the earth and the world,

*from everlasting to everlasting you are God.
You turn men back to dust,
saying, "Return to dust, O sons of men."
For a thousand years in your sight
are like a day that has just gone by,
or like a watch in the night.
You sweep men away in the sleep of death;
they are like the new grass of the morning—
though in the morning it springs up new,
by evening it is dry and withered.
We are consumed by your anger
and terrified by your indignation.
You have set our iniquities before you,
our secret sins in the light of your presence.
All our days pass away under your wrath;
we finish our years with a moan.
The length of our days is seventy years—
or eighty, if we have the strength;
yet their span is but trouble and sorrow,
for they quickly pass, and we fly away.
Who knows the power of your anger?
For your wrath is as great as the fear that is due you.
Teach us to number our days aright,
that we may gain a heart of wisdom.
Relent, O Lord! How long will it be?
Have compassion on your servants.
Satisfy us in the morning with your unfailing love,
that we may sing for joy and be glad all our days.
Make us glad for as many days as you have afflicted us,
for as many years as we have seen trouble.
May your deeds be shown to your servants,
your splendor to their children.
May the favor of the Lord our God rest upon us;
establish the work of our hands for us—
yes, establish the work of our hands.*

—Psalm 90:1-17

- Do my thoughts resemble the poem of Moses in Psalm 90 or the honesty of Job?
- How do these biblical writers' opinions resemble mine?
- What can I learn from them?
- What could I say to others who struggle in similar ways?

SAVOR

Have someone read this short story to the group. Ask the questions that follow the story.

Tim and Marie Kuck spent a Christmas in the hospital with their son Nathaniel. It was his first Christmas. They watched doctors and nurses and machines as the six-month-old child struggled to survive. As they suffered, Tim and Marie also heard their heavenly Father guide them to find ways of helping others deal with seasonal battles of sickness and sadness.

For the next three years the Kucks and many friends carried Nathaniel back to the hospital on Christmas to sing, smile, offer gifts, and pray for patients and their families. Through Nathaniel's multiple birth anomalies, surgeries, therapies, feeding tubes, and special care, the Kucks learned so much about how life really counts. Since four-year-old Nathaniel's passing to heaven on November 13, 2001, the Kucks have continued their holiday celebration of healing. Their ministry, Nathaniel's Hope (http://www.nathanielshope.org/), seeks to help families and friends realize those with disabilities really count.

(from Chris Maxwell, *Changing My Mind*)

Ask: Do you think Tim and Marie felt like Job? Why do you think they decided to trust God through their disappointment? What can we learn from them?

EXPERIENCE

"The good news is the Pursuer doesn't give up and keeps after us."

—Cecil Murphey, *The Relentless God*

Read the above quote to the class. Then ask them these questions.

- What are some examples of times when you have felt God has given up on you?
- Why is it so hard to believe he pursues us?
- How can we convince ourselves of that?

Discussion option: Show a movie clip from Bruce Almighty *(19:20–23:15—Begin as he talks at home about his anger; end after he refuses to answer his* phone by the water.) After the clip, have the group discuss the scene in relation to this session. Here are some questions to consider:

- *Does Bruce Almighty's anger toward God resemble how you view God? How is it similar or different?*
- *In what ways are you ever like Bruce?*
- *If you were in Bruce's place on the screen, what would you say?*

During the next week, write a few sentences comparing your beliefs to those found in the Web sites below. If you have your own site, describe your view of God there. If you do not have a site, e-mail a friend from this group a description of your beliefs in God.

Look into it
- Why many do not believe: http://atheism.about.com/od/doesgodexist/
- Why to believe: http://www.christianitytoday.com/cl/2000/002/6.36.html
- http://www.peterkreeft.com/audio/08_arguments-for-god.htm
- Gary Moon, *Falling for God*
- N. T. Wright, *Simply Christian*

WALK
Play Episode 4 clip from the Faith Café DVD. Ask:
- *What do Dr. Moon's comments say to you?*
- *Do you agree with him?*
- *What keeps us from moving forward and applying these ideas?*
- *What do you think Job would have said if he had been sitting beside Dr. Moon?*

There are many times in our lives when our faith in God will be challenged. Learning how others view God can remind us of and challenge us to define what we believe, why we believe it, and how we can successfully live the truth in everyday life.

"Always be prepared to give an answer to everyone who asks you to give the reason for the hope that you have."

—1 Peter 3:15

Find out others' views on a supreme being.
- Spend time with someone you don't know very well. Ask that person if he or she believes in a higher power. Have the person describe his or her views of God.

This week's spiritual discipline is reading:
We often choose to read small portions of Scripture, perhaps to save ourselves more time for staring at the thrilling pages of an exciting novel or a dramatic tale told on a TV screen. But the Bible contains stories of conflict, confrontation, drama, and discovery. This week's discipline gives us a chance to avoid letting our opinions control our decisions: make a choice to read the book of Job. Notice the honesty; observe the confusion; stay in the story. The discipline of reading through Job inspires us to endure whatever we face in life.

End your time together with a prayer that focuses on asking for God's wisdom as we examine our views of him and seek to find the truth about who he is. Ask for courage to talk to others about their views and ask to be shown opportunities for these conversations to happen. Thank God for making himself known to us through his Word and through our relationships with him.

NOTES

EPISODE 5 | OUR GOD

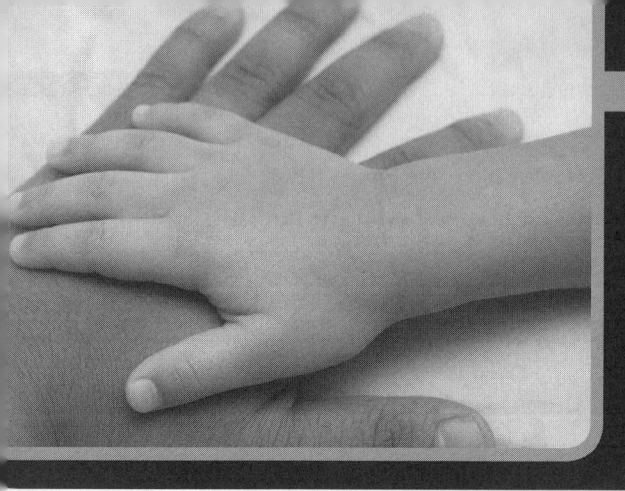

Is God My Father?

SUPPLIES NEEDED
Faith Café DVD
Chalkboard or poster board for class members to write on
Chalk or dry-erase marker
The Apostles' Creed
Paper and pens or pencils

ENTER

Begin the session with the Lord's Prayer, inviting the group to pray with you: Our Father which art in heaven, Hallowed be thy name. . . . Ask: What picture of God does that prayer bring to mind? If that Father is in Heaven with a hallowed name, how can he be your Father?

Who we are and what experiences we have lived through shape our relationship to God. Maybe you have an easy time thinking of God as your Father. Maybe this concept is foreign to you, or even anxiety-producing. Take this opportunity to reexamine this facet of your relationship with your creator.

"You can tell for sure that you are now fully adopted as his own children because God sent the Spirit of his Son into our lives crying out, 'Papa! Father!' Doesn't that privilege of intimate conversation with God make it plain that you are not a slave, but a child? And if you are a child, you're also an heir, with complete access to the inheritance."

—Galatians 4:6, 7 (*The Message*)

Spend a few moments quietly reflecting on the following questions:

- *Daddy. Heavenly Father. Almighty God.* Which name for God are you most comfortable with? Why?
- Do you believe in God? If so, how would you describe him?
- How does God compare to your earthly father?
- What is God telling you to do?
- What has God done to you when you disobeyed?
- Are you willing to change your view of God if it is not correct?

Consider it
"They expect that as a Father, he will respond to humanity, his children, acting in our best interests, even punishing those who misbehave like a father punishes his children, to restore those who trust in his love."

—from Wikipedia

Let the class discuss the quote above. Here are some conversation starters: Was your father the one who doled out punishment in your family? How did you feel about that? What did you most fear? When you think of God as our Father, do you think about him punishing us? What kind of punishment do you think you have received from God?

DRINK

Have one person read each of these passages.

Grace and peace to you from God our Father and the Lord Jesus Christ. Praise be to the God and Father of our Lord Jesus Christ, who has blessed us in the heavenly realms with every spiritual blessing in Christ.

I keep asking that the God of our Lord Jesus Christ, the glorious Father, may give you the Spirit of wisdom and revelation, so that you may know him better.

Through him we both have access to the Father by one Spirit.

For this reason I kneel before the Father.

[There is] one God and Father of all, who is over all and through all and in all.

Sing and make music in your heart to the Lord, always giving thanks to God the Father for everything, in the name of our Lord Jesus Christ.

Peace to the brothers, and love with faith from God the Father and the Lord Jesus Christ.
—Ephesians 1:2, 3, 17; 2:18; 3:14; 4:6; 5:20; 6:23

GO DEEPER

For us to obtain a better biblical view of God as our Father, we need a grasp of what Paul had in mind. As Paul wrote to the Jews, he described the creator God as more than their leader; he was their Father. In this letter, instead of emphasizing the religious efforts, customs, duties, or ancestry of the Jews, Paul focused on God's selection of them as a people. They had not earned the Father's welcome; he chose them.

Paul also hoped to educate the Gentiles about their adoption by Father God into his family. Paul wanted to reveal truth about this God who is the Father of all—no more favoring of the Jews and rejection of the Gentiles.

Can God the creator, ruler, and owner be for us, all of us, God the Father—no matter where we have come from or what we have done? Yes. Paul's letter, written to the church at Ephesus and circulated among other churches, echoes this truth along with other blessings of the Christian life. But none of that can be obtained unless the first step is taken—welcoming God the Father's welcome, accepting his acceptance. In reading this letter, Paul's audience then and today can grasp the glorious reality of God the creator being God the Father.

Life Application Notes
Letters in Paul's day would frequently begin by identifying the writer and the readers, followed by a greeting of peace. Paul would usually add Christian elements to his greetings, reminding his readers of his call by God to spread the gospel, emphasizing that the authority for his words came from God, and giving thanks for God's blessings.

God is *over all*—this shows his overruling care (transcendence). He is *through all* and *in all*—this shows his active presence in the world and in the lives of believers (immanence). Any view of God that violates either his transcendence or his immanence does not paint a true picture of God.

Holman Bible Dictionary: God
God has revealed himself as Father and Creator, as Son and Savior, and as Holy Spirit and Comforter. This has led the church to formulate the uniquely Christian doctrine of the Trinity. New Testament passages make statements about the work and person of each member of the Trinity to show that each is God; yet the Bible strongly affirms that God is one, not three (Matthew 28:19; John 16:5-11; Romans 1:1-4; 1 Corinthians 12:4-6; 2 Corinthians 13:14; Ephesians 4:4-6). The doctrine of the Trinity is a human attempt to explain this biblical evidence and revelation. It is an explicit formulation of the doctrine of God in

harmony with the early Christian message that "God was in Christ, reconciling the world unto himself" (2 Corinthians 5:19). It expresses the diversity of God the Father, God the Son, and God the Holy Spirit in the midst of the unity of God's being.

Play the Episode 5 clip from the Faith Café DVD. Discuss the Cosmic Sheriff portrayed by actor Curt Cloninger. How does that God resemble our views of God? What words did the sheriff say that got your attention? What was Cloninger teaching you about God through that drama?

Use the chalkboard or poster board to write names of God. Give the group time to suggest titles, phrases, and names that remind them of God. Think of these as starters and include them if others do not mention them or if you need to get the discussion going: Heavenly Father, Healer, Listening Ear, Holy God, King, Ruler, Supreme Being, Almighty God, Jehovah Jireh—Our Provider, God of Hope.

SAVOR

Most of us choose to admire some things and people more than others. Admiring God can mean respecting and holding a high regard for him. But would it shock you to know that he also admires you?

A personal reflection

As I was waiting in the Lord's presence, he spoke this to me: "I admire you." This, of course, made me very uncomfortable as I wrestled with this obviously being a product of my flesh. But then he clarified what he meant by a picture in my mind. He showed me a picture of a young father standing over a newborn baby's bassinet, looking at the child with eyes of admiration that only a father can understand. Then I began to understand he admires us because he is a Father, and we are his children. That baby didn't do anything to deserve the father's admiration. As a matter of fact, all he would be doing is making smelly diapers, spitting up food given so lovingly, etc. Yet the father loves, admires, and takes care of him anyway! It was truly an encouraging word in such times of unknown future as these.

(Greg Amos, Christian education leader, Lake City, South Carolina)

EXPERIENCE

Belief in God is higher in the Midwest and the South (both at 82%) than in the East and the West (both 75%). It tends to increase with age from 71% of those aged 25–29 to more than 80% for the three age groups of people over 40, including 83% of those aged 65 and over.

Women are more likely than men to believe (84% vs. 73%). African Americans (91%) are more likely than Hispanics (81%) and whites (78%) to believe in God. Republicans (87%) are more likely to believe than Democrats (78%) and Independents (75%). Those with no college education (82%) are more likely to believe in God than those with postgraduate education (73%).

Church attendance (every month or more often) is higher in the Midwest (45%) and the South (40%) than in the East (30%) and the West (27%). It is lowest among people aged 25–29 (24%) and highest among those aged 65 and over (43%). And it is higher among women (41%) than among men (31%).

Look into it
- For more information on this survey, please go to http://www.harrisinteractive.com/harris_poll/index.asp?PID=408
- http://en.wikipedia.org/wiki/God_the_Father
- Curt Cloninger, "Finding a God Who Is Big Enough" (Session One), *God Views*, LifeSprings Resources, 2003
- James R. Lucas, *Knowing the Unknowable God*
- Max Lucado, *Just in Case You Ever Wonder*

As a group take a look at the statistics stated above. Ask some of the following questions to help the class digest this information:

- *Why do you think that certain portions of our country have higher percentages of people who believe in God?*
- *What might cause women and African Americans to be more likely to believe in God than other portions of our population?*
- *If the percentages of those who believe in God are at least 75%, why is the average church attendance so much lower?*
- *Does having an accurate view of God affect someone's participation in spiritual exercises (like church attendance)? If so, how?*
- *What else stands out to you in these statistics?*

- *How does this belief influence every area of your life? How should it?*
- *What could help that happen?*

> Try these ways of living out and sharing the truth of knowing God as your Father.
>
> - Write a note to your heavenly Father. Offer him honest thoughts, feelings, appreciation, and requests.
> - Then write a letter to a friend about God's love and acceptance. Use passages of Scripture to stay on the right track. Instead of signing your name, let your friend see it as a note to him or her from God's Word about his love.
>
> **This week's spiritual discipline is worship:** Plan in advance to set aside at least ten minutes each day for only worshiping God: not in a church service or group setting, but you and God alone. Think about who he is. Do not worship the worship or let songs be at the center of your heart. Let God be. Enter a time of intimate worship of your creator.

WALK

"Dear Father, I have often become so busy in the details of my daily living that I have missed the joy of the love relationship you want to have with me. Open my mind and heart to discover the truths you want me to know. Reveal your love to me so that I understand and experience it in new and greater ways. Speak to me, dear Holy Spirit. I am listening."

—Steve McVey, *A Divine Invitation*

Repeat this portion of the Apostles' Creed:
"I believe in God the Father Almighty, maker of heaven and earth."
Have each member of the group say that several times. Say it aloud. Ask the following questions:

Before concluding, pass out paper and pens or pencils and ask all who attend the class to write a short note to their heavenly Father. Ask if anyone would like to share his or her letter to God as a closing prayer, but be ready to share your own if no one else is willing.

NOTES

EPISODE 6 | OUR GOD

What Did Jesus Do for Me?

SUPPLIES NEEDED
Chalkboard or white board
Chalk or dry-erase marker
Wrapped Christmas present

ENTER

As you begin today, ask the group to read the following quotes to themselves and sit quietly as they think about the messages these writers are trying to convey.

Jesus prayed, "I have given them the glory that you gave me, that they may be one as we are one: I in them and you in me. May they be brought to complete unity to let the world know that you sent me and have loved them even as you have loved me" (John 17:23, 24). In order for us to be clear about our relationship with God, we have to consider who Jesus is and what he has done for us.

"Neediness is a spiritual necessity. The whole point of the gospel is that we can't save ourselves!"
—Lisa Harper, *Relentless Love*

"Only one person could fill the bill, and the miracle of the cross is that he did."
—Rebecca Manley Pippert, *Hope Has Its Reasons*

"Christianity is the only religion on earth that has felt that omnipotence made God incomplete. Christianity alone has felt that God, to be wholly God must be a rebel as well as a king."
—G. K. Chesterton

Some people may think about Jesus every day. Some may only think about him twice a year, if at all.

- When do you think of Jesus most?
- What do you think of when you hear the word *holiday*?
- What images first come to your mind as you think about Easter and Christmas?
- *Birth, ministry, miracles, death, burial, resurrection.* What parts of the story of Jesus' life hold the most meaning for you?

Continue the discussion. Write the following words on the board: Christmas, Good Friday, Easter. Ask the following questions:

- *What do all three holidays have in common? (Though the answer is Jesus, allow this interaction to bring many thoughts to light.)*
- *What was the ultimate purpose behind these three events?*
- *What kinds of things have you or someone you know incorporated into your holiday celebrations to help keep proper perspective?*

Consider it
"Almost every viewer of this movie had a very strong opinion before they laid eyes on it."
—Danny Minton, on *The Passion of the Christ*, KBTV-NBC Beaumont, Texas

26 | FAITH CAFÉ

Conversation starter: How many people in the room saw the film The Passion of the Christ? *Consider the quote from the reviewer above. Reread the quote aloud, changing the word* movie *to* Christ, *and* it *to* him. *Talk about how that statement may have been true during Jesus' life on earth and how it might be true today.*

DRINK

They nailed him up at nine o'clock in the morning.
—Mark 15:25 (*The Message*)

For God so loved the world that he gave his one and only Son, that whoever believes in him shall not perish but have eternal life.
—John 3:16

GO DEEPER

Life Application Notes

Crucifixion was a feared and shameful form of execution. The victim was forced to carry his cross along the longest possible route to the crucifixion site as a warning to bystanders. There were several shapes for crosses and several different methods of crucifixion. Jesus was nailed to the cross; condemned men were sometimes tied to their crosses with ropes. In either case, death came by suffocation as the person lost strength and the weight of the body made breathing more and more difficult.

Reading the story of Christ's crucifixion reminds us of the reality. Somewhat. Watching movie imitations of the experience reveals the pain to us. Somewhat. Music, sermons, lessons, conversations, prayers, and videos—nothing really takes us there. Jesus Christ was executed by the bloody, painful, humiliating, sickening method of being nailed on a cross. The march and beatings and ridicule and cuts. The struggle to breathe. The scene of pain and desperation, the smell of death, the loneliness of the God-man Jesus dying on a cross with no miracle ordered to rescue him from the hurt. John 3:16 tells us that God loved everyone so much—that is the reason for the birth, the death, and the resurrection of Jesus. We are the reason for the seasons. For God to have us. For us to be had by God.

Engage the participants in a conversation centered on the following questions:

- What has kept us from accepting the amazing truth of Christ's death?
- What are some practical ways we could help ourselves live in the awareness of this truth? (Write the group's ideas on the board.)

SAVOR

The reading of this story could be divided up among volunteers from the group. Another idea might be to read the first half of the story and save the last half (beginning with "Oh, the beauty") to be read at the very end of class.

A group of eager youngsters converge on a playground for an after-school game of baseball. Chuck, the tallest, is in charge. . . . The competitors ready themselves with warm-up tosses and exaggerated challenges. Chuck summons the group after brief moments of preparation, informing them that he and Wilson, as usual, are the captains who will choose teams. The group has endured the process frequently. The talented, or the most popular, get picked first. The awkward hopefuls experience the humiliation of being chosen last. If at all. That's how it is for Allen.

He is overweight and uncoordinated. His thick glasses and hand-me-down clothes provide ample ammunition for taunting from the insecure peers who never ignore such a perfect target. His name is Allen. Rarely do the boys call him Allen, opting instead for jests that attack his weight, his eyesight, his clothing, or his clumsiness. So, on this day, he expects the usual round of ridicule as he suffers through the endless few minutes of rejection.

Allen, aware of his limitations, desperately longs for an opportunity, for a chance, for a friend.

Chuck chooses first. He always does. The eager candidates can easily predict the order of selection. Chuck regularly orchestrates the process to guarantee himself the upper hand. And to ensure that Wilson gets stuck with Allen.

Today, however, is different. Chuck looks relaxed. He doesn't hurry. He looks over the group several times, smiling as if he knows something they do not. Then, he shocks them all. He picks Allen. He picks Allen *first*. Not a good hitter, a good pitcher, or a good comedian. Allen. As other boys snicker, Chuck says, "I'm serious." Then he says, "Come on, Allen, I want you on my team."

Oh, the beauty of fairy tales. Underdogs win. Frogs become princes.

The story of our after-school ballplayers may not happen in our neighborhoods, but we would love for it to. . . . In the Gospels of Grace, we catch a glimpse of our dreams of glory. We see that fairy tales can come true. Jesus, this historical world shaker, claimed to espouse as his mission the releasing of the imprisoned and the loving of the unloved. He walked into the playground of the ancient eastern world and chose players for his team. His choices shocked those chosen, and baffled those observing in the stands of tradition and political correctness.

The gospel teaches, in a sense, that he has drafted each of us. Though we stand back, awkward and amazed, he hands us the bat. Though we're frogs, he kisses us. Though we're ugly stepchildren, he makes the slipper somehow fit.

He came, and comes, to give life to the lifeless.
(from Chris Maxwell, *Beggars Can Be Chosen*)

EXPERIENCE

The Apostles' Creed (Latin: Symbolum Apostolorum*), sometimes titled Symbol of the Apostles, is an early statement of Christian belief, creed, or "symbol." The Apostles' Creed is widely used by a number of Christian denominations for both liturgical and catechetical purposes, most visibly by liturgical churches of Western tradition. . . .*

The theological specifics of this creed may have been originally formulated as a refutation of Gnosticism, an early heresy. The name of the Creed comes from the fact that it, being composed of twelve articles, was earlier believed to have been written by the twelve Apostles, who each were supposed to have contributed one article.

http://en.wikipedia.org/wiki/Apostles'_Creed)

Go back through and softly repeat the Scriptures about Jesus. Pause and allow for a brief time of silence. Next, ask the group the following questions:
- *Which phrases describe something about Jesus?*
- *Why is it important to read creeds like this occasionally?*
- *What phrase or phrases remind you of a truth that you don't normally think about?*

Read the Apostles' Creed:

I believe in God the Father Almighty, maker of Heaven and earth, and in Jesus Christ his only Son, our Lord who was conceived by the Holy Spirit, born of the virgin Mary, suffered under Pontius Pilate, was crucified, dead, and buried. He descended into hell. The third day he rose again from the dead. He ascended into Heaven and sits at the right hand of God the Father Almighty, from whence he shall come to judge the quick and the dead. I believe in the Holy Spirit, the holy catholic [universal] church, the communion of saints, the forgiveness of sins, the resurrection of the body, and life everlasting. Amen.

Look into it
- Walter Wangerin Jr., *The Book of God*
- *The Passion of the Christ*, 20th Century Fox, 2004
- *The Visual Bible: The Gospel of John*, 2003

WALK

Every day our attention is drawn to a thousand things. Most of us would probably have to admit that we spend too little time thinking about Jesus. But if we want to understand him more, that's exactly what we need to do—spend time with Jesus.

We often forget what matters most, don't we? Biblical history and Christian tradition offer us experiences to remember. For example, baptism teaches and reminds us about the washing, the cleansing, and the arising as a new person in Christ. Communion remembers Jesus' death and God's covenant. Taking Communion helps us remember the price Jesus paid to receive us.

It is very important that we allow ourselves the opportunity to take in the significance of things like Communion. Encourage dialogue among the group by asking the following questions: How can we better prepare ourselves to participate in holy Communion? Are there things we can incorporate into our regular lives?

Finally, hold up the wrapped present. Discuss why we give gifts. Encourage the class to spend time this week reflecting on what they've learned about Christ, and challenge them to share him by giving a gift to someone who doesn't expect it.

> How can we help one another think of Christmas and Easter at unexpected times?
> - Ask God whom in your group you could encourage this week.
> - Consider sending a fellow participant a Christmas card or an Easter basket, just to remind him or her about Jesus.
>
> **This week's spiritual discipline is meditation:**
> Prepare daily for the next time you receive Communion by slowly reading and rereading John 3:16: Meditate on the death of Christ and the command to remember his death until he returns. Allow each phrase of that verse to flood your mind and heart. Consider replacing the phrase "the world" with your own name. For example, "God so loved John that he gave his one and only Son. . . ." Finish this time of Christian meditation by thanking God for his great and overflowing love.

NOTES

EPISODE 7 | OUR GOD

Can God Live in Me?

SUPPLIES NEEDED
Mirror
Faith Café DVD
Paper and pens or pencils

ENTER
"The world had changed."
—Opening line, *Lord of the Rings: The Fellowship of the Ring*, 2001

After Jesus ascended into Heaven, his followers obeyed his instructions. They waited. Christ had completed his time on earth. But the Holy Spirit was coming to dwell within the lives of Christ's followers. The world had changed. And it was about to change even more. Think about how you might be part of that change now.

It's your turn to be on the crew of *Extreme Makeover: Home Edition*. Imagine you've just found out Jesus is coming to live in your house next week.

- What room renovations would you tackle first?
- What would you keep the same?
- What would be the "special project" for you—something you'd want to redesign on your own and keep secret until the last minute?

"Christ has no body now but yours,
No hands, no feet on earth but yours,
Yours are the eyes through which
   he looks compassion on this world,
Christ has no body now on earth but yours."
                 —attributed to Teresa of Avila

Pass the mirror around again as you read the Consider it *quote. Remind the participants that each face looking back reveals a place where God has chosen for his Spirit to dwell.*

Consider it
"The love of God for his elect, having descended from on high and overcome every obstacle, has poured itself into the deep bed of our regenerated hearts. And to this he adds the grace of making the soul understand, drink, and taste of that love."
—Abraham Kuyper, *The Work of the Holy Spirit*,
www.ccel.org

DRINK
In my former book, Theophilus, I wrote about all that Jesus began to do and to teach until the day he was taken up to heaven, after giving instructions through the Holy Spirit to the apostles he had chosen. After his suffering, he showed himself to these men and gave many convincing proofs that he was alive. He appeared to them over a period of forty days and spoke about the kingdom of God. On one occasion, while he was eating with them, he gave them this command: "Do not leave Jerusalem, but wait for the gift my Father promised, which you have heard me speak

30 | FAITH CAFÉ

about. For John baptized with water, but in a few days you will be baptized with the Holy Spirit."

So when they met together, they asked him, "Lord, are you at this time going to restore the kingdom to Israel?"

He said to them: "It is not for you to know the times or dates the Father has set by his own authority. But you will receive power when the Holy Spirit comes on you; and you will be my witnesses in Jerusalem, and in all Judea and Samaria, and to the ends of the earth."

—Acts 1:1-8

Ask these questions:
- *What have you been told over the years about this passage of Scripture?*
- *How have you understood what Jesus meant when he talked about receiving power when the Holy Spirit comes?*

Emphasize to the class that Jesus said his Spirit would come, and those who receive him are to be witnesses locally and globally. The plan is to reach the world with truth. That goal can be accomplished as Christ's followers receive his strength through the Spirit.

When the day of Pentecost came, they were all together in one place. Suddenly a sound like the blowing of a violent wind came from heaven and filled the whole house where they were sitting. They saw what seemed to be tongues of fire that separated and came to rest on each of them. All of them were filled with the Holy Spirit and began to speak in other tongues as the Spirit enabled them.

—Acts 2:1-4

GO DEEPER

Discuss these two scenes from Acts with the participants. The first scene tells the promise from Christ about the Spirit's coming. Then in Acts 2 we read of its happening. Ask:

- If you had been the disciples, would this have been what you expected after hearing Christ's promise?
- How would you have felt if you had been there with the disciples in that place?

The promise of Christ came true! God's Spirit fell upon God's people. They did not have to accomplish world evangelism with their own talent. God would do the work through them as he gave them the strength of his Spirit.

God's Spirit—the third person in the Trinity—is God. Not just a friend of God or a product of God's plan. The Spirit is God: God-on-the-move, God-in-his-people, God-to-empower. That is the Holy Spirit. Like wind, the Spirit came. Like fire, the Spirit burned in brilliance to bring light, to burn the junk, to discard the useless effort of religious fervor, and to give the experience of the living God. That was for them then. And that Spirit is for all Christ's followers today.

"They were all filled with the Holy Ghost, more than before. They were filled with the graces of the Spirit, and more than ever under his sanctifying influences; more weaned from this world, and better acquainted with the other. They were more filled with the comforts of the Spirit, rejoiced more than ever in the love of Christ and the hope of heaven: in it all their griefs and fears were swallowed up. They were filled with the gifts of the Holy Ghost; they had miraculous powers for the furtherance of the gospel. They spake, not from previous thought or meditation, but as the Spirit gave them utterance."

—from Matthew Henry Commentary, Concise Edition

It may be helpful to think of things this way: God did more than pick us for his team. He left it up to us to make the decision about joining that team. As we've learned in these lessons, he paid for each of us to become a part of his team. He worked out every detail. But he wants us to decide.

What if we joined his team but really couldn't play the game he instructs us to play? That wouldn't feel so great, would it?

That isn't the end of the story. God not only gave Jesus to pay the price so we could join his team, but he also offers us the strength needed to follow his instructions. He offers the Holy Spirit to enter our personal lives so that the impossible becomes doable. God *in* us, not God only *above* us watching to see how we play, can do the impossible, and we can win this game of life.

SAVOR

This story helps give an understanding of what God's Spirit is to Christ's followers.

Helen Keller's parents looked for a teacher who could work with their daughter. They found the perfect fit in a nineteen-year-old orphan, Anne Sullivan. She accepted the assignment of teaching Helen, who was six and had been unable to see, hear, or speak since she was nineteen months old. Anne entered Helen's life and changed it forever. Helen no longer had to try to find ways to live. She had a guide, a teacher, and a helper.

God knows we cannot obey him on our own. He sent the Guide, the Teacher, the Helper. His Spirit can enter our lives and change us forever.

Anne surely helped Helen. With a manual alphabet and hours of training, Helen soon learned to read and write in Braille. By the time she was ten, Helen learned sounds by placing her fingers on Anne's larynx and sensing the vibrations. Anne later spelled out lectures to Helen, who became a student at Radcliffe College. Speaker, author, and one who offered hope to those who were blind and deaf, Helen could not have done any of it without Anne's hand, her voice, and her help.

After Anne died in 1936, Helen wrote this about her friend: "My teacher is so near to me that I scarcely think of myself apart from her. I feel that her being is inseparable from my own, and that the footsteps of my life are in hers. All the best of me belongs to her; there is not a talent or an inspiration or a joy in me that has not been awakened by her loving touch."

(Van Morris, Mount Washington, Kentucky; source: *Helen Keller, The Story of My Life*)

EXPERIENCE

As we seek to understand more about who the Holy Spirit is, the best place to start is in Scripture.

"But the Counselor, the Holy Spirit, whom the Father will send in my name, will teach you all things and will remind you of everything I have said to you."
—John 14:26, 27

Ask the group:
- *Can God really live in your life?*
- *If we believe this, how can we act more as if it is a truth to us?*
- *Describe people who are filled with God's Spirit, without including worship styles or events in church services as criteria; think about at home, at work, and all alone.*

Share the following story with your group:
Curt could not believe what he saw. Walking beside the broken pews, seeing the damaged carpet, looking through the cut walls, he felt sick. He asked himself, How could anyone do this to God's church?

He called the elders and deacons to give them the news. The police told him that three other church buildings had been damaged recently. They all shook their heads and wondered who could do such a thing.

As Curt walked around the church property, he felt God reminding him of something he had been teaching his people. "We are the body of Christ; this building isn't," he had told them over and over. "God's Spirit came to live inside us, not in a temple made by men." Curt knew then how God wanted him to use this disappointment. He would tell them that though a building was damaged, God's church can still do what she is called to do!

After you read this story, discuss the following questions as a group:
- *How would you describe your feelings about the damaged church building and the lessons Curt learned?*
- *If you were going to preach what Pastor Curt planned, how would you explain it to the people?*

Play Episode 7 clip from the Faith Café DVD. After viewing the clip, ask:
- Are you looking for reasons to live?
- Have you searched for life's true direction? Describe ways that God's "living in you" answers the question.
- How can the Holy Spirit turn your life around and help you and those around you to smile?

Look into it
- Find text on the Holy Spirit at www.ccel.org
- Russ Lee's site at www.russlee.com
- J. I. Packer, *Keep in Step with the Spirit*
- Billy Graham, *The Holy Spirit*

WALK

If we believe God's Spirit has come to empower Christ's followers to be witnesses of his message, the world will change.

O Holy Spirit, pour forth the fullness of your gifts . . . Renew your wonders in this our day as by a new Pentecost. Through your Word and by the power of your Holy Spirit, transform our lives so that Christ is seen in all we do, say, and think.

Empower us by humbling us before the cross of Christ.
Empower us by teaching us how to think with your wisdom.
Empower us by the power of your grace.
Empower us with the spirit of gratitude.
Empower us with the fire of the Holy Spirit.
Empower us with your love,
In the name of the Father, the Son and the Holy Spirit. Amen.
(a prayer of Pope John Paul XXIII)

Hand out paper and pens or pencils. Give the group members time to make their list of the ten ways things will be different now they have been reminded that God's presence is inside them. When they have finished, ask them to share a few of the points they listed as part of your prayer time together. Remind them that you, as the leader, are always available to pray with them as they seek to rely more on the Spirit's power in their lives.

If you are a Christian, but have never consciously welcomed the Spirit to empower you, do that before seeking to follow any lists.
- Thank God daily for allowing his presence to live in your life.
- Make a list of ten ways your life will be different now that you celebrate God's presence in you.
- Welcome God's Spirit into your inner world. Think of one area of your thoughts or feelings that perhaps you have been reluctant to let God touch. Turn that area over to him in prayer.

This week's spiritual discipline is waiting:
This waiting isn't the same as putting things off. Waiting on God is a choice to remove our thoughts and actions from our usual distractions. Waiting can be a spiritual discipline when one sits alone near God—and waits. Maybe for something. Maybe for nothing. Schedule an appointment this week to find a good location and sit in stillness. The disciples waited for God's Spirit to invade. Not such a bad idea, is it?

NOTES

EPISODE 8 | OUR GOD

Can God Use Me?

SUPPLIES NEEDED
Chalkboard or white board
Chalk or dry-erase marker
Faith Café DVD

ENTER

As we think about how God can do something of value through our lives, let us listen to the advice of those who have gone before us. Paul the apostle knew about failure and wrong choices. He also knew about experiencing God's love, acceptance, and forgiveness. Let's read his words and receive this truth.

Write these Top Ten resolutions on the board to prepare for an opening time of reflection and discussion:

1. Lose weight.
2. Quit smoking.
3. Stick to budget.
4. Save more money.
5. Find a new job.
6. Become more organized.
7. Exercise more.
8. Be more patient.
9. Eat better.
10. Become a better person.

These common goals and resolutions are not bad ideas. Most of us need to exercise and eat better. Becoming more organized is a great suggestion for many people. But look at number 10: "Become a better person." Many people seek that goal but fail to ever reach a place of "being better." How does it work?

We've investigated biblical truth about God living in us. If God is living in us, we should view ourselves as God's dwelling place, as vessels for God to live an amazing life through our weak selves. Maybe this should be number 1 on the list of resolutions: "Realize that God now lives inside my life and can change this world through me. I must let him."

> Think of what would be on your Top Ten list of resolutions you have made for yourself. Take a moment to jot your list down.
> - How many of the items on your list are things you have worked at achieving?
> - How many of the items on your list are things you have invited God to work on in you?

Consider it
"I believe God made me for a purpose, but he also made me fast. And when I run, I feel his pleasure."
—Eric Liddell, from *Chariots of Fire*

Talk about the quote above. Ask: What does that quote mean to you?

DRINK

Or didn't you realize that your body is a sacred place, the place of the Holy Spirit? Don't you see that you

can't live however you please, squandering what God paid such a high price for? The physical part of you is not some piece of property belonging to the spiritual part of you.
—1 Corinthians 6:19 *(The Message)*

He used the apostles and prophets for the foundation. Now he's using you, fitting you in brick by brick, stone by stone, with Christ Jesus as the cornerstone that holds all the parts together. We see it taking shape day after day—a holy temple built by God.
—Ephesians 2:20, 21 *(The Message)*

Paul wrote about doctrine and beliefs in his letters. He clearly stated truth about followers of Christ not living in isolation, but functioning as a corporate team, each part crucial for the whole. Since we've learned that God's Spirit can dwell in each of us, can we imagine seeing that Spirit teeming through all believers to fulfill God's goal to change the world?

GO DEEPER

The biblical doctrine is very practical in this week's passages; Paul made it all personal.

Have different students read each of these phrases. Allow time to discuss meaning. Encourage them to reread the sentences and put their names where it says "you."

- You yourselves are God's temple, and God's Spirit lives in you.
- Your body is a temple of the Holy Spirit.
- You are not your own.
- The whole building is joined together and rises to become a holy temple in the Lord.
- You are the temple of God.
- God himself is present in you.
- Remember that your bodies are created with the same dignity as the Master's body.
- Your body is a sacred place, the place of the Holy Spirit.
- The physical part of you is not some piece of property belonging to the spiritual part of you.
- He's using you, fitting you in brick by brick, stone by stone, with Christ Jesus as the cornerstone.
- We see it taking shape day after day—a holy temple built by God.

Play first Episode 8 clip from the Faith Café DVD.

At the conclusion of the clip, guide a discussion about how Paul's comments are very different from those in the clip. God, as he works through individuals and the corporate body of Christ, does not turn people into clones. As he fits people brick by brick, he allows each part to be unique and significant!

Ask: In what ways are we tempted to place God in a box? How can we make sure we keep him out?

SAVOR

There are smells, and then, there are smells! I prefer some smells to others. Freshly baked bread, a pot roast cooking in the oven, scented candles, and a newly mowed lawn, just to name a few. Then there are those "other" smells. The ones we try to avoid, like garbage, sewage, annoyed skunks . . . you get the picture.

As my toddler approached me, I could tell he needed my assistance with one of those "other" smells. "Mommy," he said, sporting a coy expression, "could you change me?" I'll spare you any further adjectives regarding the transaction that followed. But I will share his response once I finished the job: "Thank you, Mommy. Thank you for changing me." This may come as a surprise, but during their toddler years, each of my children has thanked me for changing them! Thinking of their sincere appreciation still warms my heart.

My current toddler's gratitude brings a smile to my face. Like his older siblings, he realizes his predicament. Additionally, he knows that any attempt to remedy it on his own would only bring further mess. So he comes to me.

As humans, we can get ourselves into some pretty stinky situations. Sometimes, we take a wrong turn (or two) and end up stuck in a ditch on a less than desirable road. Our Father God watches and waits. Not wanting any to be misled, he pauses to hear our cry. "Uh, God, will you change me? I am so tired of being in this mess I have made. Please change me, God."

He does not turn his ear from that cry. No good father could. "I waited patiently for the LORD; he turned to me and heard my cry. He lifted me out of the slimy pit, out of the mud and mire; he set my feet on a rock and gave me a firm place to stand" (Psalm 40:1, 2).

Think over the times in your life when God has rescued you. Maybe you got into a wrong crowd, a wrong relationship or a wrong lifestyle. You called on God, and he lifted you out and set you down on a "firm place." Thank him for that. Thank him for changing you.

Or, maybe you find that you are still on that road. You're just not ready to give up that way of life. Just be honest with God. He'll meet you where you are. He knows the mess you're in (he smells it!). But he's waiting on you.

(Mary DeMent, "Giving Thanks," used by permission)

EXPERIENCE

Discuss with the class what Frederick Buechner wrote in the following quote, about knowing the will of God for our lives. Read his quote aloud to the class. It helps us gain a better grasp of how each of us really can be used by God as we match longings with opportunities.

"The kind of work God usually calls you to is the kind of work (a) that you need most to do and (b) that the world most needs to have done. If you really get a kick out of work, you've presumably met requirements (a), but if your work is writing TV deodorant commercials, the chances are you've missed requirement (b). On the other hand, if your work is being a doctor in a leper colony, you have probably met requirement (b), but if most of the time you're bored and depressed by it, the chances are you have not only bypassed (a) but probably aren't helping your patients much either. . . . The place God calls you to is the place where your deep gladness and the world's deep hunger meet."

—Frederick Buechner,
Wishful Thinking: A Theological ABC

Use a chalkboard to draw the lines Buechner wrote about. Draw one column from the top left to the bottom right to display the work a person needs to do. Draw another column from the top right to the bottom left to display the work this world needs to have done. Inform the class that where the lines intersect illustrates the place God would have us serve him.

Emphasize this line again: "The place God calls you to is the place where your deep gladness and the world's deep hunger meet." Ask:
- *How can we become more aware of our deep gladness?*
- *How can we discover the world's deep hunger?*
- *Why do most of us live without pursuing such opportunities?*
- *What can you personally do to take the right paths?*
- *How can we support one another?*

Look into it
- Mindy Caliguire, *Discovering Soul Care*
- Larry Crabb, *Connecting: Healing Ourselves and Our Relationships*
- Rick Rusaw and Eric Swanson, *Living a Life on Loan*
- *Chariots of Fire*, Warner Home Video, 2005

Play the second Episode 8 Faith Café DVD clip. With the group, take time to discuss how this is not the true way God works through us. Although the clip is funny, think of the seriousness of it. Guide the participants toward clear thoughts that move them away from viewing God in such a false perspective. Direct the discussion with questions such as these:

- *In what ways does the video feel real to you?*
- *Is God like that?*
- *If not, how is he different?*
- *Tell us a story from your personal experience to reveal such a view of God.*
- *How can we avoid those perspectives?*

WALK

Choose this week to serve by making another Top Ten list—listing some of the "bricks" that need to be added or changed in you to become a "holy temple." God has called you for such a time as this!

"Be kind, for everyone you know is facing a great battle."

—Philo of Alexandria

Make sure your bricks are placed on a sure foundation and aren't just part of a facade.

- Stop pretending. Start doing.
- Stop lying. Speak the truth in love.
- Stop complaining. Start working at making things better.

This week's spiritual discipline is accountability:

All followers of Christ are on the same team. None of us should do this alone. Accountability—helping one another walk through the journey correctly—is a vital part of this spiritual experience. Pursue a relationship with someone who won't gossip, but will offer advice and prayer or just listen to your goals. Try to meet and pray together twice this week. Don't expect perfection from the other person or yourself. Just be a friend who is honest.

NOTES

EPISODE 9 | OUR WORLD

What Happens at Home?

SUPPLIES NEEDED
Faith Café DVD

ENTER

After we tend to our packed schedules, come home for dinner, and pay our bills, what happens? How do we be the people God wants us to be at home?

Begin by welcoming the participants into a "family gathering." Go around the room and ask each one to give his or her name, prefaced by a familial title such as aunt, father, sister, grandfather, etc. Have the participants briefly explain how they feel about being part of a family. Use the questions in the box below to guide the discussion. Encourage humor to set the stage so the class will be relaxed. Ask two or three to tell funny but brief stories of what they remember from family events that always brought laughter. Most of the conversations that follow will be serious, so we need for moods to be welcoming and calm.

Think of your childhood. Think of holidays, vacations, conversations, games, arguments, laughter, and hugs. Think of today.

- What words describe your family?
- Who are the members of your real family? Are you close to them?
- How well does your family know you? How well do you know them?

Consider it
- 44% of adults say that having a satisfying family life is their highest priority in life.
- 18% of people said that completely understanding and carrying out the principles of their faith was the highest priority in their lives.

—from a 2005 Barna Research poll, www.barna.org

Have a quick discussion about these statistics (above). When might these two sets of priorities conflict? Which do you think have to be met first?

DRINK

Before you read these passages aloud, tell the "family" it is time for a devotional, and you plan to read biblical instructions about how a family should operate.

Get rid of all bitterness, rage and anger, brawling and slander, along with every form of malice. Be kind and compassionate to one another, forgiving each other, just as in Christ God forgave you.
—Ephesians 4:31, 32

Submit to one another out of reverence for Christ. Wives, submit to your husbands as to the Lord. For the husband is the head of the wife as Christ is the head of the church, his body, of which he is the Savior. Now as the church submits to Christ, so also wives should submit to their husbands in everything.

Husbands, love your wives, just as Christ loved the church and gave himself up for her to make her holy, cleansing her by the washing with water through the word, and to present her to himself as a radiant church, without stain or wrinkle or any other blemish, but holy and blameless. In this same way, husbands ought to love their wives as their own bodies. He who loves his wife loves himself. After all, no one ever hated his own body, but he feeds and cares for it, just as Christ does the church—for we are members of his body.

—Ephesians 5:21-30

Fathers, do not exasperate your children; instead, bring them up in the training and instruction of the Lord.

—Ephesians 6:4

Fathers, do not embitter your children, or they will become discouraged.

—Colossians 3:21

*Our children and their children
will get in on this
As the word is passed along
from parent to child.
Babies not yet conceived
will hear the good news—
that God does what he says.*

—Psalm 22:30, 31 (*The Message*)

*Point your kids in the right direction—
when they're old they won't be lost.*

Proverbs 4:3, 4 (*The Message*)

*When I was a boy at my father's knee,
the pride and joy of my mother,
He would sit me down and drill me:
"Take this to heart. Do what I tell you—live!"*

—Proverbs 22:6 (*The Message*)

Then little children were brought to Jesus for him to place his hands on them and pray for them. But the disciples rebuked those who brought them.

Jesus said, "Let the little children come to me, and do not hinder them, for the kingdom of heaven belongs to such as these." When he had placed his hands on them, he went on from there.

—Matthew 19:13-15

Ask the "family" the following questions:
- *Which passage was your favorite? Why?*
- *Are there any you wish weren't in the Bible? Why?*
- *How do you feel after hearing or reading those passages?*

GO DEEPER

In today's passages we see the biblical image of family life. Paul wrote about parents and their discipline and training of children. But he warned readers not to use parental authority incorrectly. Our modern world needs to read Paul's note again. All around us we see two extremes: on one side is the kind of family where discipline and correction are nonexistent; on the other side, we still see verbal and physical abuse. And can't we also label departure from families as a type of abuse? Family life today is threatened by broken relationships.

The proverbs promote parental wisdom and guidance. The text from Matthew 19 broadcasts a time when Jesus got into trouble. It was not politically correct for a leader like Christ to be involved in the lives of children. However, he held them and sent a message to his audience. He still sends that message today: "Jesus said, 'Let the little children come to me, and do not hinder them, for the kingdom of heaven belongs to such as these.' When he had placed his hands on them, he went on from there."

Paul knew that marriages could be lived out in the biblical pattern of love: being willing to die to self and live for another. And Paul knew correction could come without exasperating or embittering children. But Paul also knew that the secret to having good family relationships was the same as the secret to having any kind of successful relationship—treating others with kindness and compassion, and being willing to forgive and ask forgiveness. Do we know that? God wants today's families to change the statistics and set examples of his true love in action.

SAVOR

Read or have someone read this story out loud. Then answer the questions that follow.

The kids secured their bike helmets and prepared to leave. It had been a great day at the park, but the clouds were closing in fast. I knew we needed to leave immediately if we intended to remain dry all the way home. The last thing I wanted was a brisk stroll in the rain with two preschoolers and an infant in tow. So I urged them to pick up the pace.

My oldest son led the way; I followed, pushing the baby in the stroller. And my three-year-old daughter was right behind us. At least I *thought* she was right behind us. I turned around and saw that she was lingering inside the park fence. I motioned for my oldest son to wait. Then I hurried back to gather my daughter. There she was, leisurely picking wild flowers. "Here, Mommy, I picked these for you," she said in her cute, little-girl voice.

Dark clouds hovered directly over our heads. Thunder sounded in the distance. A light drizzle began to fall. And my daughter was picking flowers. I shook my head and placed her firmly on her bike. "To obey is better than sacrifice!" I reprimanded.

As the verse left my lips, I understood it for the very first time.

On any other occasion, I would welcome my daughter's "sacrifice" of flowers. However, flowers were not what I needed at that moment.

She bypassed my instructions in order to please me. However, her plan failed. I was not pleased. Instead, I was angered. I couldn't fully appreciate her gift while concerned about her safety.

Sometimes we act like three-year-olds. We attempt to please God with our "sacrifices" and offerings. We reason that, if we do this or that, he will be delighted. We neglect his commands and carry on with our *own* game plan. God is not pleased. Saul feared man. Consequently, he chose to modify God's orders to his own liking. "But Samuel replied, 'Does the Lord delight in burnt offerings and sacrifices as much as in obeying the voice of the Lord? To obey is better than sacrifice, and to heed is better than the fat of rams. For rebellion is like the sin of divination, and arrogance like the evil of idolatry" (1 Samuel 15:22, 23). By circumventing God's plan, we are, in essence, like Saul, saying we know more than God. God desires obedience.

Is there a storm brewing in your life? Are you facing a major decision? Whatever your position, listen to that "still, small voice" of God. He wants to lead you safely Home.

(from Mary DeMent, "Heading Home," used by permission)

Discuss the following questions with the group:
- What have you "picked up" when the time wasn't right?
- How have many of us suffered through "storms" because we did not let others in the family "take us home"?
- What "little drizzles" bring the most damage in today's families?
- Discuss ways family relationships cause storms in life and ways families can help members endure and learn from storms.
- How is God part of it all?

EXPERIENCE

"According to Foster, submission does not demand self-hatred or loss of identity. Instead, it simply means growing secure in the conviction that 'our happiness is not dependent on getting what we want' but on the fulfillment that naturally flows from love of one's neighbors. Such wise and encouraging suggestions have helped many readers to discard the idea that discipline is an onerous duty and to move toward a liberating and simpler idea of discipline—whose defining character, as Foster never forgets, is joy."

—reviewer Michael Joseph Gross on Richard Foster's *Celebration of Discipline*

Play Episode 9 clip 1 from the Faith Café DVD. At the conclusion of the clip, engage the group in dialogue about their own memories of family. Ask these questions:
- What did she say that reminds you of your family memories?

- *How do you wish your family had been different?*
- *What are some specific suggestions you could share about bringing family values in line with biblical principles? (Guide them toward practical principles, not toward a political discussion. Encourage each one that we can change family dynamics by applying our beliefs at home.)*

Look into it
- William F. Harley Jr., *His Needs, Her Needs*
- Dr. Kevin Leman, *Bringing Up Kids Without Tearing Them Down*
- Dr. Henry Cloud and Dr. John Townsend, *Boundaries*
- www.family.org
- www.familylife.com
- www.fln.org
- www.marriagebuilders.com/index.html
- www.fathersforlife.org/divorce/chldrndiv.htm

LOOK FURTHER

We want to offer you a warning. First, about the facts we plan to supply. They are scary and painful facts about what has happened to families in today's society. They might frighten you and your class. Remind the audience that we hear bad news every day, but today we plan to study this "bad news" for good reasons.

Next, we warn you because the information is true. It hits our hearts directly. Maybe our own lives are packed with such pain. We all know relatives and friends who live in painful places called "family." Rather than avoiding it, we believe this study can offer information as it dares us to do something and make a positive difference. Read the following statistics to the class.

The following statistics come from the e-newsletter *Common Sense & Domestic Violence*, [1998 01 30] (found on http://www.fathersforlife.org/divorce/chldrndiv.htm, where the original sources of the data are cited):

For the best part of thirty years we have been conducting a vast experiment with the family, and now the results are in: the decline of the two-parent, married-couple family has resulted in poverty, ill-health, educational failure, unhappiness, anti-social behavior, isolation and social exclusion for thousands of women, men and children.

Nearly two of every five children in America are living without their fathers in the home.

From fatherless homes come . . .

63% of youth suicides.

90% of all homeless and runaway children.

85% of all children who exhibit behavioral disorders.

80% of rapists motivated with displaced anger.

71% of all high school dropouts.

70% of juveniles in state-operated institutions.

85% of all youths sitting in prisons.

To look at the facts in a slightly different way, a child from a fatherless home is . . .

4.6 times more likely to commit suicide.

6.6 times more likely, if a girl, to become a teenaged mother.

24.3 times more likely to run away.

15.3 times more likely to have behavioral disorders. 6.3 times more likely to be in a state-operated institution.

10.8 times more likely to commit rape.

6.6 times more likely to drop out of school.

15.3 times more likely to end up in prison while a teenager.

Compared to children who are in the care of their two biological, married parents, children in the care of single mothers are 33 times more likely to be abused seriously enough to require medical attention, and 73 times more likely to be killed.

WALK

Play the second Episode 9 Faith Café DVD clip. Invite the participants into a discussion about Steve Ely's comments:
- *Which of his statements impacted you the most?*
- *How do modern families fail to understand the status of today's youth?*
- *What can families do to change that?*
- *What can we do to change it?*

Contact some of your relatives this week. Ask the Holy Spirit to direct your decisions about whom to write or call. Pray for each member of your family or close friends every day this week. Make steps toward forgiving family members who have hurt you, and accept God's forgiveness for your past mistakes.

Allow the class time to talk briefly about each point in the following box. End the discussion by reminding the group that none of us will always be successful in living this way. Give them a few moments to confess silently and accept God's forgiveness for past mistakes related to families. Complete the prayer by allowing them to forgive family members who have hurt them.

If you have no family near you, view this list as advice for your close relationships.
- Pray as a family and pray separately.
- Say what should be said and remain silent when the words could bring damage.
- Display true Christian character at home.
- Play together and laugh; have fun and go to ball games, concerts, mountains, or beaches.
- Stay together by not giving up; be determined to endure, commit, and hope.

This week's spiritual discipline is submission:
We often panic when we hear this word. However, its misuse does not give us a reason to remove it from the Bible or our lives. To whom will you submit this week? How can that process inspire your relationship with your heavenly Father?

NOTES

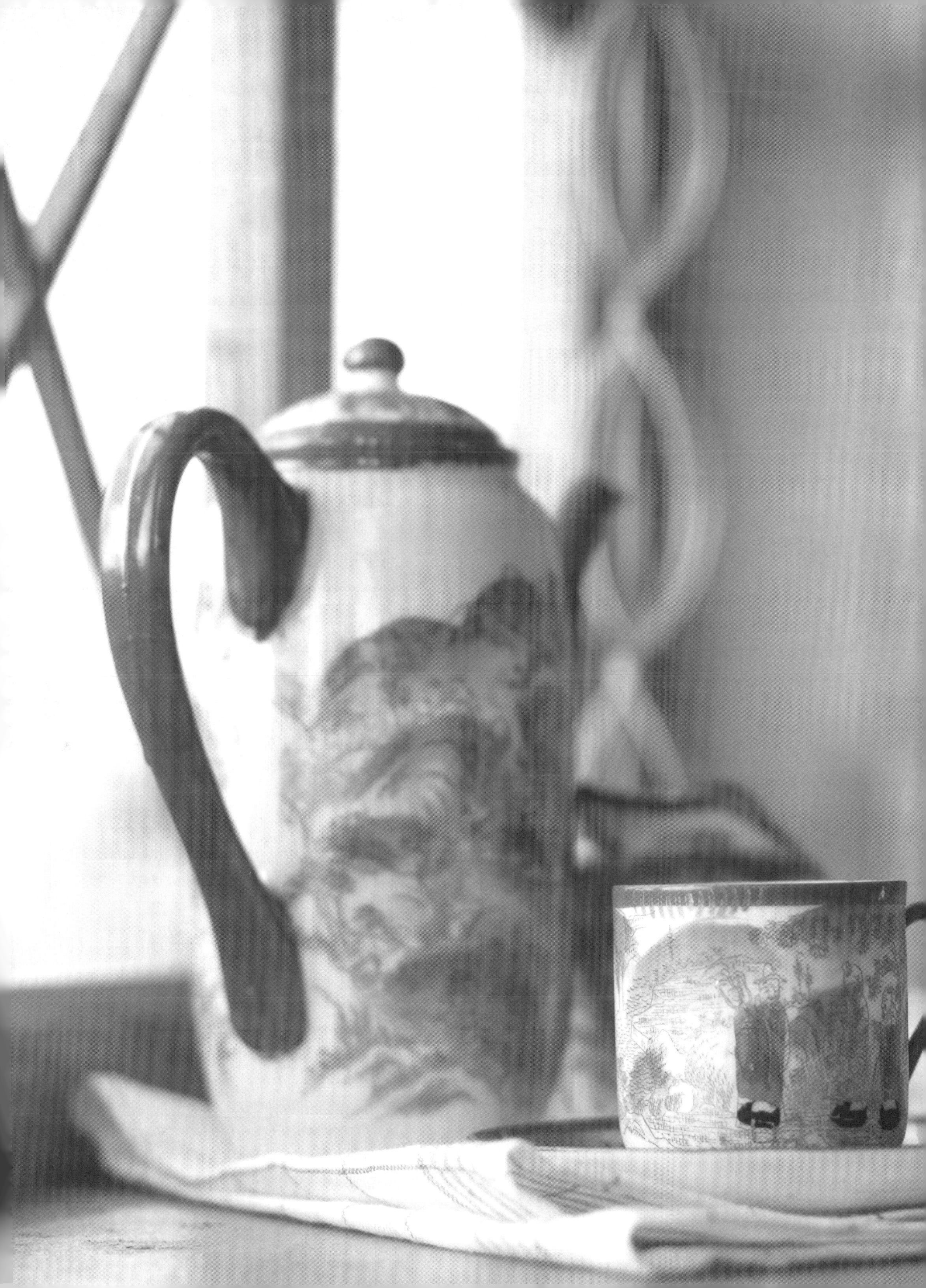

EPISODE 10 | OUR WORLD

What Happens at Work?

SUPPLIES NEEDED
Faith Café DVD
Chalkboard, white board, or poster board
Chalk, dry-erase marker, or other marker

ENTER
Whether you're a stay-at-home parent or a nine-to-five cubicle inhabitant, doing your job—doing it well and in a way that would please God—can be a challenge. How do we live the life God wants for us at work?

"When we set out to hear God's voice, we do not listen as though it will come from somewhere above us or in the room around us. It comes to us from *within*, in the heart, the dwelling place of God."
—John Eldredge, *Waking the Dead*

"I find that doing the will of God leaves me no time for disputing about his plans."
—George MacDonald

Begin the class by having each participant explain his or her job. There are some suggestions for discussion questions in the box below.

Then move to the Consider it *discussion: Many people are probably familiar with sayings similar to the John Wooden quote. Usually we associate this type of quote with the idea of doing a job well. But what if we thought of it in a different light? What if we thought of it in relation to our witness about God to our coworkers? What if it was about our relationship with God?*

Describe a day in your work life.
- What time do you arrive at work?
- How far do you drive?
- What mood are you usually in before, during, and after work?
- What do you wear?
- How close are you to your coworkers?
- Is this what you dreamed of doing?

Consider it
"If you don't have time to do it right, when will you have time to do it over?"
—John Wooden, former UCLA basketball coach

DRINK
Therefore, as God's chosen people, holy and dearly loved, clothe yourselves with compassion, kindness, humility, gentleness and patience. Bear with each other and forgive whatever grievances you may have against one another. Forgive as the Lord forgave you. And over all these virtues put on love, which binds them all together in perfect unity.

Let the peace of Christ rule in your hearts, since as members of one body you were called to peace. And be thankful. Let the word of Christ dwell in you richly as you teach and admonish one another with all wisdom, and as you sing psalms, hymns and spiritual songs with gratitude in your hearts to God. And whatever you do, whether in word or deed, do it all in the name of the Lord Jesus, giving thanks to God the Father through him.
—Colossians 3:12-17

44 | FAITH CAFÉ

SAVOR

Have different people in the group take turns reading this story Jesus told of the sheep and goats.

When he finally arrives, blazing in beauty and all his angels with him, the Son of Man will take his place on his glorious throne. Then all the nations will be arranged before him and he will sort the people out, much as a shepherd sorts out sheep and goats, putting sheep to his right and goats to his left.

Then the King will say to those on his right, "Enter, you who are blessed by my Father! Take what's coming to you in this kingdom. It's been ready for you since the world's foundation. And here's why:

I was hungry and you fed me,
I was thirsty and you gave me a drink,
I was homeless and you gave me a room,
I was shivering and you gave me clothes,
I was sick and you stopped to visit,
I was in prison and you came to me."

Then those "sheep" are going to say, "Master, what are you talking about? When did we ever see you hungry and feed you, thirsty and give you a drink? And when did we ever see you sick or in prison and come to you?"

Then the King will say, "I'm telling the solemn truth: Whenever you did one of these things to someone overlooked or ignored, that was me—you did it to me."

Then he will turn to the goats, the ones on his left, and say, "Get out, worthless goats! You're good for nothing but the fires of hell. And why? Because—

I was hungry and you gave me no meal,
I was thirsty and you gave me no drink,
I was homeless and you gave me no bed,
I was shivering and you gave me no clothes,
Sick and in prison, and you never visited."

Then those "goats" are going to say, "Master, what are you talking about? When did we ever see you hungry or thirsty or homeless or shivering or sick or in prison and didn't help?"

He will answer them, "I'm telling the solemn truth: Whenever you failed to do one of these things to someone who was being overlooked or ignored, that was me—you failed to do it to me."

Then those "goats" will be herded to their eternal doom, but the "sheep" to their eternal reward.

—Matthew 25:31-46 (*The Message*)

GO DEEPER

Jesus was a great teller of stories. He used the stories (parables) to do more than get his audiences' attention. His goal? To present truth. To see lives changed. To reveal reality.

As he spoke to this group of listeners, he told a tale each could picture in his or her mind. The listeners knew about sheep and goats, so Jesus voiced truth about actions of love proving (not earning, but proving) spiritual authority by using those animals as his actors. The sheep illustrated believers; the goats, unbelievers. His audience knew that sheep and goats stayed near each other until it was time to shear the sheep. Jesus emphasized their similarities and their differences; he highlighted their eternal separation, just as a shepherd separates the sheep from the goats.

His point? Christians should take care of people in need. As individuals care for others and prove their care by acts of love, those actions are actually being done to Christ. Whatever Christians do for others, they are actually doing to him.

The result? Eternal blessings for those who bless Christ by blessing people in need. Salvation is not earned by doing, but proof of true faith is what believers do unto others. Jesus demanded personal involvement in caring for the needs of people.

Christ's story was a warning. He hoped to keep all from eternal punishment. His story was also an invitation. He welcomed all who would become a part of his flock.

"Why sheep and goats? God often describes his people as sheep in Scripture. Sheep listen to their shepherd and follow him. They look to him for all their needs and will suffer without him. What are goats like? Goats are stubborn. They resist being told what to do. They'll eat (take in) almost anything, even garbage. People who please God do what he says and look to him for guidance. People who resist God and want to do their own thing are stubborn, and end up accepting the lies and garbage of this world. The goats in the lesson thought they were doing God's work, but they were obviously not listening to how he wanted it done, or they were doing it for their own goals, not his. He didn't even know them."

—from http://www.ebibleteacher.com/children/lessons/sheepgoats.htm

After discussing sheep and goats, talk with the class about the importance of service. It is easier to criticize a speaker's message than to actually apply what was taught. Maybe he or she didn't voice it just right. Maybe he or she quoted the wrong passage, forgot the third point of a sermon, or called a biblical character by an incorrect name.

Is God bothered more by those things or by our failure to apply his truth? Does the Sunday morning dress code and lighting influence this world more than feeding the hungry and visiting the sick?

When congregations gather together, the event is often called a "church service." Let that remind us that God wants churches to be "in service," not only in corporate gatherings of worship and sermons and prayer. God is telling today's followers to take truth "to go." On Mondays, church services can happen in offices, factories, restaurants, and fields as Christians live out Christ's teachings at their places of work. Every day is an opportunity for us all—for *you*—to make this world a better place.

Faith Café is all about the "to go" of our beliefs. If truth is of value, it must go with us wherever we go. Ask:

- *What keeps us from taking our Christian beliefs to work?*
- *Can you describe an experience with a coworker who set a good example of his or her faith in God on the job?*
- *What made that person different?*
- *What steps can you take to let your faith have more of an impact in your work life?*

EXPERIENCE

"Be very careful, then, how you live—not as unwise but as wise, making the most of every opportunity, because the days are evil. Therefore do not be foolish, but understand what the Lord's will is."

—Ephesians 5:15-17

Whether at home, in the fields, in an office, or on a turnpike, you have the opportunity each day to live like Jesus and show his light to those around you. Don't miss it! Find resources that help you make the most of your working hours.

Look into it
- www.leaderslighthouse.com
- www.christianadvice.net/christianity_at_work.htm
- www.christiansatwork.org.uk/cgi-bin/caw.cgi
- www.christatwork.org/templates/System/details.asp?id=22809&PID=64231
- Rob Briner, *Roaring Lambs*
- Mark Greene, *Thank God It's Monday*

Play Episode 10 clip from the Faith Café DVD. Give the class time to discuss the interview with Richard Foster. Ask:

- *How does this clip fit today's discussion?*
- *Why is it important to live out true commitment in everyday life?*

WALK

Acts of service can remind us of what God did for us. Didn't Jesus say that whatever we do for others is what we actually do for him? Seek ways to serve Jesus in this coming work week.

Take some time at the beginning of your work day to talk to God: *Father, you have placed me in this position. Forgive me for missing so many opportunities to make a positive difference. Speak through me and love through me. Make my world better as you work through me at work. In Jesus' name, Amen.*

Ask the participants to take out and hold up their business cards if they have them. (Not everyone will have a card; instruct those individuals without cards to lift their hands, pretending to hold up something that describes their work environment.) For those who stay at home or attend school, remind them of the importance of viewing wherever they are as a mission field. As the group members hold up their cards or just their hands, take time to pray for them.

As a group, find a few ministries in your area that offer services to those in need and plan to work on a project together. Get involved. Challenge and be challenged.

- Serve food to the hungry.
- Plan a clothing drive.
- Visit people in a nursing home.

This week's spiritual discipline is service: Service is often viewed as a duty rather than a spiritual discipline. Jesus set a much different example. He gave and cared. He looked for ways to prove his love for others. Think about how people have helped you and served you. Come up with wild ideas for "doing good unto others" at work. Be willing to serve in ways you've never served before. Serve by doing, even when no one will know who served.

NOTES

EPISODE 11 | OUR WORLD

What Happens at Church?

SUPPLIES NEEDED
Paper and pens or pencils
Faith Café DVD

ENTER

"Life occurs between people as well as within them."

—Nathan Schwartz-Salant, *The Mystery of Human Relationship*

"Let us not give up meeting together, as some are in the habit of doing, but let us encourage one another."

—Hebrews 10:25

What about the people sitting beside you? Do you know them? Do they know you?

Think about what might happen if we worked together to apply our spiritual principles in a corporate body of true friends—not just those who sometimes act like friends, but those who choose to become friends because of sharing forgiveness and redemption by the same blood: the blood of Christ.

Jesus shed his blood for all. Keeping this truth in mind will provide us with a better perspective on how our beliefs should work in the church environment.

Pass out paper and pens or pencils to the group. Using the questions below, lead the participants in a discussion about their church experience.

Let's think about our church experience.

- Make a list of some things you don't like about church.
- Make a list of things you do like about church.
- What lessons do you think God is trying to teach you through your church experience?
- How should you respond to the challenges you face so God is honored?
- In what ways can you help to make Christ's body where you are alive, active, and growing?

Consider it

"People go to church for the same reasons they go to a tavern: to stupefy themselves, to forget their misery, to imagine themselves, for a few minutes anyway, free and happy."

—Mikhail Bakunin, Russian philosopher

Consider it discussion: Have you ever felt like the quote above could be true? Do you think there are people who go to your church for those reasons? What would you say to someone who believed that to be true? What would you say to someone who was going to church for those reasons?

48 | FAITH CAFÉ

DRINK

Just as each of us has one body with many members, and these members do not all have the same function, so in Christ we who are many form one body, and each member belongs to all the others. We have different gifts, according to the grace given us. If a man's gift is prophesying, let him use it in proportion to his faith. If it is serving, let him serve; if it is teaching, let him teach; if it is encouraging, let him encourage; if it is contributing to the needs of others, let him give generously; if it is leadership, let him govern diligently; if it is showing mercy, let him do it cheerfully.

—Romans 12:4-8

Paul wrote to a group of leaders who struggled to agree. Grace, rules, methods of worship, who does what—all are issues with which today's church is still grappling. Here Paul chose to highlight the variety of gifts while stressing the importance of teamwork. We need to remember to do that today.

GO DEEPER

Read the Scripture below to the group. Before you do, ask each one to keep paper and pen or pencil handy so they can jot down any thoughts that stand out from this passage. Or ask them to keep track of how many times Paul uses the word "one."

The body is a unit, though it is made up of many parts; and though all its parts are many, they form one body. So it is with Christ. For we were all baptized by one Spirit into one body—whether Jews or Greeks, slave or free—and we were all given the one Spirit to drink.

Now the body is not made up of one part but of many. If the foot should say, "Because I am not a hand, I do not belong to the body," it would not for that reason cease to be part of the body. And if the ear should say, "Because I am not an eye, I do not belong to the body," it would not for that reason cease to be part of the body. If the whole body were an eye, where would the sense of hearing be? If the whole body were an ear, where would the sense of smell be? But in fact God has arranged the parts in the body, every one of them, just as he wanted them to be. If they were all one part, where would the body be? As it is, there are many parts, but one body.

The eye cannot say to the hand, "I don't' need you!" And the head cannot say to the feet, "I don't need you!" On the contrary, those parts of the body that seem to be weaker are indispensable, and the parts that we think are less honorable we treat with special honor. And the parts that are unpresentable are treated with special modesty, while our presentable parts need no special treatment. But God has combined the members of the body and has given greater honor to the parts that lacked it, so that there should be no division in the body, but that its parts should have equal concern for each other. If one part suffers, every part suffers with it; if one part is honored, every part rejoices with it.

Now you are the body of Christ, and each one of you is a part of it. And in the church God has appointed first of all apostles, second prophets, third teachers, then workers of miracles, also those having gifts of healing, those able to help others, those with gifts of administration, and those speaking in different kinds of tongues. Are all apostles? Are all prophets? Are all teachers? Do all work miracles? Do all have gifts of healing? Do all speak in tongues? Do all interpret? But eagerly desire the greater gifts.

And now I will show you the most excellent way.

—1 Corinthians 12:12-31

Ask the class what were the last major or even minor purchases they made. Invite a few people to share their stories about their shopping process and whether or not they were pleased with the end result. Ask:

- *How can coming to the church with a consumer mentality hurt the body of Christ?*
- *How do members in today's body of Christ sometimes work against one another to get the best "deal," instead of working together?*
- *Without inappropriate gossip, have a few participants tell stories about what they've seen happen that hurt others in churches.*

Play Episode 11 clip from the Faith Café DVD. Invite the group to relax and worship together as a church (a group of Christ's followers).

SAVOR

Read or have others read the story. Then read the Scripture that follows.

As my obstetrician warned me about the baby's place, I feared the birth of our next child. We did not have insurance, and the cost of complicated work would be a lot. As the doctor expressed risks associated with our options, comfort did not come to me. I wasn't sure what to do next.

Of course, I asked people to pray. But did I really mean it? Believe in it? Pray myself? Or is "pray for me" just something I tend to say in times of unrest? While these questions circled my already disoriented brain, a handful of women expressed their urge to intercede for me. Each mentioned that thoughts of my unborn child's positioning woke them up in the middle of the night and prompted them to prayer. Thank God! One felt led to gather together, pray and lay hands on me, as instructed in James 5:14. At least one felt led to fast and did so on my behalf. Another stopped praying and began thanking God for the work she knew he would do. Wow! So, knowing that, I walked into my next doctor's appointment confident that the baby had turned, right? Wrong.

Besides the doctor, no one was more surprised when the doctor said, "Well, the head is down. The baby turned." I lay there frozen. What? "It must have been all of those prayers," he said smiling. Then his face turned serious. "I have to admit," he said, "I did not think this baby was going to turn."

Prayer. I've read several books on the subject. I observe it. And I can pinpoint countless references in Scripture urging us to practice it. Still, sometimes, I just do not understand how it works. Is that really necessary, though? As I think about it, there are several technological items I use but fail to totally grasp their inner workings. My failure to fully understand does not prevent me from embracing them on a daily basis.

What is going on in your life? Is there something you desire God to turn around? Maybe it's a disobedient child or a distant spouse. Maybe it's a job or financial situation. I do not know your need. But I do know that God is able to turn lives in a different direction. Just as he literally turned my son around in my womb, he is more than able to turn your life, your circumstances around. Though you and I may not totally comprehend it, he uses the avenue of prayer, our conversations with him, to accomplish that goal. And he likes it when we invite others into our lives to join us in prayer.

(Mary DeMent, "Turning Point Prayers," used by permission)

"If my people, who are called by my name, will humble themselves and pray and seek my face and turn from their wicked ways, then will I hear from heaven and will forgive their sin and will heal their land. Now my eyes will be open and my ears attentive to the prayers offered in this place."

—2 Chronicles 7:14, 15

EXPERIENCE

"Ninety-eight percent of U.S. churches have fewer than 300 in attendance on any Sunday morning; 85 percent of these experience a net loss or no net gain in membership each year; 2,000 new churches are started each year; 6,000 are closed permanently."

—Sweet, McLaren, and Haselmayer, *A Is for Abductive: The Language of the Emerging Church*

Look into it
- www.religion-online.org/showarticle.asp?title=1723

And there is no question that it has become a widespread plague in our postmodern society.

In the midst of this epidemic, a growing group of Christian trend-watchers have decided that the dropout crisis is actually a move of God. They claim that the Holy Spirit is reordering the church and bringing us back to more of a New Testament model, recalling a simpler era when Christians met "house to house" (see Acts 2:46) and did not waste time or money on religious buildings or nonessential church programs.

So now we have a touchy debate brewing. The proponents of house churches have positioned themselves against the "traditionalists," a category that includes pastors of mega-churches, leaders of media ministries, anyone who is a member of a denomination, and anyone who attends a congregation that is too big to fit into a coffee shop or a living room.

I got involved in the debate two months ago when I wrote a not-so-flattering review of George Barna's book *Revolution*—which encourages Christians to leave churches and discover the pastor-your-own-church-in-a-coffee-bar version of Christianity. I stepped into the fray and said what I still believe today: Barna has made a dangerous proposal. He says we need innovation, but what he is advocating is spiritual anarchy.

As soon as that column was posted on our Web site, the hate mail began to pour in. These "revolutionaries," a lot of whom are grinding heavy axes because they were mistreated in churches five years ago, began swinging their blades in my direction. One guy even predicted that *Charisma* will soon shut down (leaving me without a job) because everyone will be in house churches and won't need a Christian magazine.

At the risk of sounding like a rigid traditionalist, I beg to differ with Barna even though I agree with many of his conclusions. Of course Christians do not have to meet in religious buildings on Sunday mornings to "have church." Of course most ministry should happen outside the church walls. I've been saying that for years, and a lot of the congregations I preach to assemble in civic buildings, office parks, and hotels.

I am 100 percent in favor of innovation, and I believe we must constantly employ creative strategies to reach our generation for Christ. But I do not agree that innovation requires us to discard the need for godly, New Testament authority.

Many of the people who want to see traditional churches closed down and padlocked are the ones who tend to flit from one church to another, sowing discord and speaking against appointed servant-leaders. When these mavericks' pride or false doctrines are challenged, they move to another church. Are these the kind of people we want to lead a new grassroots movement?

No, thanks. Regardless of where my church meets, I intend to hold on to the New Testament principles of healthy, accountable leadership.

What about you? I'd love to hear what you think about the house-church debate. Do you believe traditional churches should disband? Have you left your church to join an "organic" church that meets in a home? If so, what was it about your traditional church that triggered your departure? I hope to share some of our readers' responses in a future column.

—J. Lee Grady, "Christian Dropouts and the Coming 'Revolution,'" from Fire in My Bones

J. Lee Grady is editor of Charisma and an award-winning journalist. To read his first column on George Barna's book Revolution, go to www.fireinmybones.com/01-17-06/. Article used by permission.]

Take the question Lee asks and make it personal. What about us? Discuss specific ways today's church families can be spiritually alive without departing from the wonderful tradition of congregational settings. And as individuals, what can each of us do to help our churches fulfill God's plan for us rather than disbanding? How can each of us personally choose to make things better instead of complaining about how they are?

WALK

How can your group make your local church even better? Be creative and think out loud of things that this smaller body can do, not by demanding that things be changed in a certain way, but by loving people, praying, caring, serving, and using spiritual gifts to make a huge difference.

Some ideas:
- Send a card to or visit a church member who is sick. Decide to make this a regular activity.
- Volunteer to greet people at the next service.
- Think of a talent or gift that you have and name one way this could be used to serve the church.

This week's spiritual discipline is celebration:
Celebration is not about just doing what we like to do. Spiritual celebration is choosing to rejoice because of God—not only for what he has done for us, but more for who he is. It involves praise and worship, reverence and awe, excitement and intimacy. Choose to celebrate God in various settings this week. As you celebrate, make sure you do not let what you like or dislike about worship styles get in the way of you and God. God wants you to honor him. So do it.

NOTES

EPISODE 12 | OUR WORLD

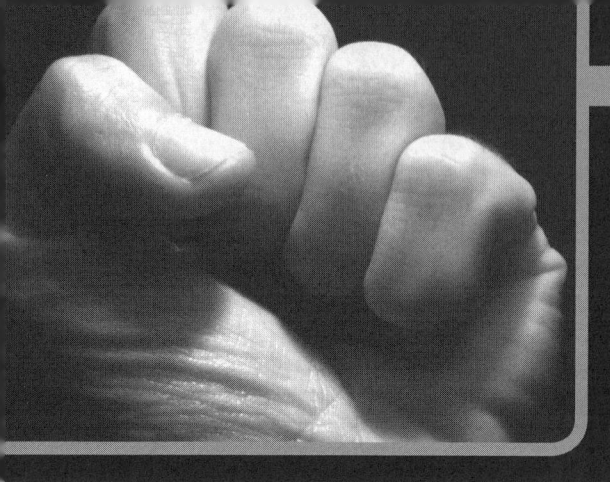

What Happens with My Enemies?

SUPPLIES NEEDED
Chalkboard, white board, or poster board
Chalk, dry-erase marker, or other marker
Faith Café DVD

ENTER
We've talked about family and church and careers. We've learned about God's will for our relationships with siblings, coworkers, and church members. But what about those we hate? What about those who hate us? What about nations we are now at war against?

We don't have to love them, do we? *Do we?*

Let's plan a strategy for attack. The first step is to identify our enemies.

- Who do you see as enemies of our country? of Christians? of your own family?
- Why are these groups or persons considered enemies?
- What could be done to change your view of them as enemies?

Consider it
"Father, forgive them; they don't know what they're doing."

—Luke 23:34 (*The Message*)

Play Episode 12 clip from the Faith Café DVD. Follow up with these questions:
- Why did Stormie hold on to her hurt for so long?
- What helped her to forgive?
- How are we like her?
- What can we do to make things better?

Put a list on the board of those in Scripture who were willing to forgive. Read the passages and discuss each story briefly.
- *Esau forgives Jacob.*
  Genesis 33:4, 11
- *Joseph, his brethren.*
  Genesis 45:5-15; 50:19-21
- *Moses, the Israelites.*
  Numbers 12:1-13
- *David forgives Saul.*
  1 Samuel 24:10-12; 26:9, 23; 2 Samuel 1:14-17
- *David forgives Shimei.*
  2 Samuel 16:9-13; 19:23; 1 Kings 2:8, 9
- *Solomon forgives Adonijah.*
  1 Kings 1:53
- *The prophet of Judah forgives Jeroboam.*
  1 Kings 13:3-6
- *Jesus forgives his enemies.*
  Luke 23:34

Encourage the group to put themselves in the places of these biblical figures. Ask:
- Why did they forgive those who caused pain?
- How could emotions have kept them from forgiving?
- How do those ancient narratives compare to our own battles? What is similar?
- Can these stories help us become more willing to forgive?

54 | FAITH CAFÉ

DRINK

When a Samaritan woman came to draw water, Jesus said to her, "Will you give me a drink?" (His disciples had gone into the town to buy food.)

The Samaritan woman said to him, "You are a Jew and I am a Samaritan woman. How can you ask me for a drink?" (For Jews do not associate with Samaritans.)

—John 4:7-9

"You have an enemy. He is trying to steal your freedom, kill your heart, destroy your life."
—John Eldredge, *Waking the Dead*

The hostility between Jews and Samarians had developed centuries before this moment when Jesus stopped at the well. The customs and religious practices of the Samaritans were different from the Jews, and the Jews considered this people to be a mixed race and inferior to them. They did not associate with the Samaritans at all, if they could help it. In fact, rather than using the shortest route from Judea to Galilee, which went through Samaria, the Jews would make a long detour around the area. But Jesus was different. He led his disciples straight through, no doubt revealing more to them than just a short cut.

We must realize that the people we struggle to like are not the real enemy. The Bible teaches that Satan is our foe. People, even those who act in hateful ways, are loved by God. This session is designed to help us remember the identity of our true foe and choose to display Christ's character to those around us. Even the ones we may dislike we can choose to treat with honor.

If time allows, read the GO DEEPER section to the group.

GO DEEPER

Alone and worn from his journey, Jesus sat by a well. His robe flashed no religious logo. A woman approached to draw water.

The middle of the day was a strange time for her to undertake this task. People habitually took care of such business before the sun became their enemy. Gathering in the morning or evening hours made the climate work in their favor, as labor turned into an arena for conversation. They socialized as they worked.

Not that woman. She came during the heat of the day, revealing her standing with society. Enduring the relentless afternoon sun was better than suffering the silence of a condemning group gathered around a well.

Jesus was not put off by her presence. In fact, his choosing to not leave when she drew near underscored the first dynamic of evangelism illustrated by this story: Jesus broke the rules.

Devout Jews despised the people of Samaria. Jesus didn't. He refused to allow man's religious rules to hinder his purpose. Travel through a sinful city? Converse with a woman? A Samaritan woman? A Samaritan woman known for her wicked ways? Such acts were never done.

Except by Jesus. He came to do the will of his Father without concern for religious or social tradition. Children, sinners, prostitutes, thieves, poor, uneducated people—he touched all those ignored by religious rule-keepers.

The clean hands of strict legalists would not dare applaud his efforts. But he continued. And he reminded listeners of his purpose: "It is not the healthy who need a doctor, but the sick. I have not come to call the righteous, but sinners to repentance" (Mark 2:17).

Jesus remained on course despite strong winds of Pharisaical opposition that sought to blow him in another direction. He broke rules; they judged him guilty by association. Their muttering confirmed that he remained true to his agenda: "This man welcomes sinners and eats with them" (Luke 15:2).

Eating with people during Christ's day carried social significance. Christ embraced people others avoided. He associated with the guilty to reach them, not to become like them. But in order to reach them, He first entered their world.

(Chris Maxwell, *Beggars Can Be Chosen*)

SAVOR

My friend and I browsed through a bookstore. I struck up a conversation with the store manager. He seemed friendly and eager to know more about us. Halfway through our conversation I told him we were both pastors.

He was shocked. Not because he doesn't like ministers, but because he'd never really had a decent conversation with a Christian. "I normally only hear from Christians when they are mad," he told us.

The three of us sat down at the coffee bar. The manager told tales about religious people who had called, written or walked in his store to inform him they would never do business with him because of objectionable books or Halloween displays.

The man thanked us for being different and then excused himself so he could get back to work. My thoughts were racing so fast I found it hard to finish my bagel. No bestseller could have taught us what we learned from that honest man.

I asked my friend, and myself, "How can believers shine a light and promote the gospel in a sinful, wicked world?" Maybe God wants people today to follow the example of Jesus. Time and technology have changed, but yesterday's techniques can still touch today's world.

Sitting idly as silent witnesses isn't enough. Lumbering ahead to peddle words without the Spirit is too much. We need to reach the world as Jesus did. He models a personal, realistic approach to speaking forth the good news. Let's stare at him again. Let's discover the steps Christ used to initiate conversation with the people he met, and open the door for true evangelism.

(Chris Maxwell, *Beggars Can Be Chosen*)

Ask the class if anyone has ever had a similar interaction with a non-Christian as what was described in the story. What was the result? What do they think? If they were not believers, would they be drawn to or repelled by the Christians they have known?

EXPERIENCE

Read the quote below. Dr. Martin Luther King Jr. knew about conflict and adversity. However, he still chose to pursue greatness rather than comfort or convenience. Think of the conflict he endured, and ask:
- *In what specific ways did he pursue his purpose in spite of the pain?*
- *What other people have walked through adversity and made our world a better place?*
- *Who has helped you personally?*
- *Where would we be today if those people had chosen convenience?*
- *What can we learn from their endurance?*

"The greatness of a man cannot be seen in the hours of comfort and convenience, but rather in the moments of conflict and adversity."

—Dr. Martin Luther King Jr.

What does it mean to forgive the enemies who seek to destroy us? As you watch, read, or listen to the news this week, think about what forgiveness could look like.

Look into it
- www.scu.edu/ethics/publications/ethicalperspectives/spohn.html
- Hal Donaldson, *Midnight in the City*
- John Ortberg, *The Life You've Always Wanted*

WALK

"Reading the daily paper can, in conjunction with journaling, be a conscious time of prayer for the world. We may write of our concern for earthquake victims, our fear of nuclear disaster, our joy at a new birth or a peace accord. As we journal in response to the daily news, we interact with what is happening in the world; we feel more strongly the connections between ourselves and others around the globe."

—Anne Broyles, *Journaling: A Spiritual Journey*

As you read the news this week, think of Jesus' response to his enemies. Jesus broke rules by hanging out with those his custom told him to avoid. But he loved them and loves us too much to play a political game. All people are those Christ loves. All people are those for whom Christ died.

Commit to a strategy for dealing with your enemies this week—not out of hatred, but out of love.

- Write letters of kindness, encouragement, or forgiveness.
- When you talk and disagree with someone, consciously decide to end the conversations with love.
- Watch the news at least one night. See those toward whom you and your country feel hatred. Choose to intercede for those your nation fights against. Pray, asking God to remind them of his love.

This week's spiritual discipline is confession:

Who have you wronged? Who have you hated? It is time to ask for forgiveness. Do not justify your behavior or rationalize its occurrence. Read this prayer aloud: "Forgive us our debts, as we also have forgiven our debtors" (Matthew 6:12).

Now tell God you are sorry. Ask him to forgive you and to help you not to act badly toward others. Receive his forgiveness. And, for those times when the others know you have wronged them, confess to them and ask to be forgiven.

"Often I realize in the middle of the process that I have not taken the time to ask for God's help or even simply stopped to spend time with him, to gaze into his face."

—Michael Card, *Scribbling in the Sand*

NOTES

EPISODE 13 | OUR WORLD

How Far Does This Go?

SUPPLIES NEEDED
Chalkboard or white board
Chalk or dry-erase marker
List of church-supported missionaries

ENTER

"I ran and ran and ran every day, and I acquired this sense of determination, this sense of spirit that I would never, never give up, no matter what happened."
—Wilma Rudolph, runner, U.S. gold medalist in 1960 Olympics

Have your group reflect on the following thoughts and questions either silently or corporately:

How do we respond to that urge to which Wilma Rudolph referred? Our life shouldn't be all about achieving our own accomplishments. But neither is life about just knowing biblical truth. The reality of our beliefs comes out in how we run the race. And the true spiritual victory comes as we serve others.

How do we—how can we—run toward a spiritual victory every day? Think about these questions.

- What do I need to leave behind in order to run most effectively?
- How can I be sure my path is straight?
- Where do I believe God wants me to go?

Consider it
"If the fields are white for harvest, why do we spend all our money on painting the barn?"
—C. Thomas Davis, *Fields of the Fatherless*

Divide the class into two groups. Have each group on its own explain what this quote means. Then have one group argue for spending resources on "painting the barn" and one argue for spending resources on the "harvest."

DRINK

If anyone would come after me, he must deny himself and take up his cross and follow me. For whoever wants to save his life will lose it, but whoever loses his life for me will find it.
—Matthew 16:24, 25

We are God's workmanship, created in Christ Jesus to do good works, which God prepared in advance for us to do.
—Ephesians 2:10

He said to them, "Go into all the world and preach the good news to all creation."
—Mark 16:15

Peter replied, "Repent and be baptized, every one of you, in the name of Jesus Christ for the forgiveness of your sins. And you will receive the gift of the Holy Spirit. The promise is for you and your children and for all who are far off—for all whom the Lord our God will call."
—Acts 2:38, 39

58 | FAITH CAFÉ

Ask the group:
- *What do these verses make you think or feel?*
- *Do the words make you want to go and do what the speakers say to do?*
- *Do you think the command to "go" and "preach" was meant for you?*
- *Why or why not?*

GO DEEPER

Jesus did what no one else could do. He paid the price. Through his blood, the sins of all can be forgiven.

The problem? Christ's followers are the ones selected to speak and live that truth. Jesus voiced the assignment as instructions to go. He was saying, "The green light is on. Do not get stuck where you are. I've called you to spread the news of my death and resurrection. I love those people near you. I love those people far away. Please, as my Spirit empowers you, team with others in our family and tell them the truth they long to know."

Jesus instructed them to tell the gospel, the good news. Isn't it an amazing opportunity to be called by God to tell such news? Discuss the following questions:

- What holds us back from going to new places?
- Do any of you feel guilty for not going to places where others are willing to go?
- Rather than guilt, what would God have us feel, think, and conclude?
- Isn't it possible to change the world even if we cannot physically travel to other countries?

Those words of Christ from Mark 16:15 stand among Jesus' final statements. His closing remarks should spark us all to be those who fulfill the calling he placed. As we do so, the desperate world finally hears the truth.

Life Application Notes

Jesus told his disciples to go into all the world, telling everyone that he had paid the penalty for sin and that those who believe in him can be forgiven and live eternally with God. Christian disciples today in all parts of the world are preaching this gospel to people who haven't heard about Christ. The driving power that carries missionaries around the world and sets Christ's church in motion is the faith that comes from the resurrection. Do you ever feel as though you don't have the skill or determination to be a witness for Christ? You must personally realize that Jesus rose from the dead and lives for you today. As you grow in your relationship with Christ, he will give you both the opportunities and the inner strength to tell his message.

SAVOR

Fran traveled to Guatemala and displayed acts of kindness to poor people who have never heard the gospel. Jim flew to Mexico to help a mission organization build church auditoriums. Michael drove to New Orleans to repair damage from Hurricane Katrina. Marsha knows that her role as a hospital nurse is about much more than the medical condition of her patients or the policies and procedures of her staff; she views each day as a ministry opportunity. Karen was not hired by a local congregation for a full-time ministry position, but she found a job and spends as much time as possible helping to encourage children and ladies in a church setting. Richard left his well-paying job to take on a ministry; he and his family serve breakfast and lunch to street people and hookers five days a week. Marvin knew God had bigger plans for him than his high-paying career and his status in the financial market; he chose to care for people that everyone seemed to ignore.

Each of those followers of Christ took their beliefs seriously. They lived them. They displayed the doctrine by actions. Outside of church auditoriums, in schools, in hospitals, on foreign land, and in nearby homeless shelters, the possibilities for influencing the world are many. Our lesson's question is legitimate: How far does this go? The answer, if we hold to biblical strategies, is this: *to the ends of the earth.* But the answer—since we are now the ones called by God to live and voice his love to others—is really this: *as far as we will take it.*

The gospel will go as far as we can go. That doesn't mean the same thing for all of us. Each one is called to use his or her gifts and experience to display God's truth to those needing it. Rather than just sermons and corrections, instead of formalities and formulas, let's all choose to voice the gospel in acts of kindness locally and globally. Start nearby. Be willing to travel to foreign soil if directed by God. But wherever God leads, find joy in the task of fulfilling the Great Commission.

Encourage your group to think about ways they can participate in Jesus' Great Commission (Mark 16:15). Ask yourself and the rest of the class the following questions:

- *Have you been on a mission trip?*
- *What did you learn?*
- *What did you have to fight through to convince yourself to go?*
- *Where do you believe God wants you to visit some day?*
- *What is stopping you?*

EXPERIENCE

There are all kinds of ways to support the spreading of the gospel, even without leaving your house. As you read and look at the resources listed below, think about how each ministry displays what all of us should seek to do in some way. Speaking truth in the language of every tribe. Reaching those who are not yet reached. Showing videos and telling stories to bring truth to people. Traveling to other countries. Learning how to think locally and globally. Realizing that those with disabilities are in desperate need of our message of truth.

Look into it
- http://ccci.org
- http://www.ywam.org
- http://wycliffe.org
- http://tcci.org
- http://nathanielshope.org/
- Bob Briner, *Roaring Lambs*
- Elisabeth Elliot, *Through Gates of Splendor*
- Patrick Johnstone, *Operation World: When We Pray God Works*
- C. Thomas Davis, *Fields of the Fatherless*
- John Piper, *Don't Waste Your Life*

WALK

"Simple acts of kindness are all it takes to change a life, a community, even a nation."
—C. Thomas Davis, *Fields of the Fatherless*

At work, at home, at the store: choose to notice those around you. Do not judge them or look down on them. Realize God has called you to shine his light of love to them. Allow his reflection to shine.

Consider ways your group could be involved in short-term missions.
- Financial support
- Prayer partnering
- Communicating with missionaries
- Planning and going on trips
- Telling the gospel message

This week's spiritual discipline is journeying:
Journeying means going somewhere, meeting someone, or doing something we rarely do, with the single motive of showing God's love to someone else. Take time this week to travel down streets you normally ignore. Get to know someone new. Through your journey you may take the truth farther than you ever have.

"Preach the gospel at all times—if necessary, use words."

—Francis of Assisi

Close the session by reading the quote above and praying. Ask the group to spend some time in silent prayer, asking God for help with whatever issues might be holding them back from telling the gospel, with or without words. Conclude the prayer by thanking God for the missionaries currently serving him and asking for their protection.

NOTES

Soul Health

You can't be fruitful if you neglect the soul

by Mindy Caliguire

Yesterday, I stood in front of a ministry team and asked, "What tends to emerge in the life of a person who neglects his or her soul? What symptoms creep in?"

I explained that no one ever sets out to trash the condition of his soul. Yet we often find ourselves in a spiritual death spiral. But we march dutifully onward, assuming that our spiritual state, a neglected soul, is somehow part of the "deal."

So I asked, "What are the signs of soul neglect?" At first the room was silent. Then somebody ventured, "Anxiety," and I knew they got it (not every group does). Once started, their answers came so fast I couldn't write them on the flip chart fast enough. "Self-absorption," they called out, along with "shame," "apathy," "toxic anger," "chronic fatigue," "lack of confidence," "isolation," "sin looks more appealing," "no compassion," "self-oriented," "drivenness," "loss of vision," and "no desire for God." Soon every inch of the page was crammed.

A sad feeling hovered over the room as these leaders saw themselves in the mirror.

Then, with much relief, we turned the page, and I asked, "What emerges in your life when you're deeply connected with God, when your soul is healthy?"

This page also filled up quickly: "love," "joy," "compassion," "giving and receiving grace," "generosity of spirit," "peace" (at this point, some bright bulb usually suggests the entire list of the fruit of the Spirit!), "ability to trust," and "discernment."

Heads nodded in acknowledgment as individuals recalled times when this was their experience too. All in all, a pretty desirable list.

Then I brought it to a vote. Holding up the Soul Neglect list, I asked, "Who votes for this?" Everyone laughed! No one in his right mind would choose to live this way. Then I called their bluff. "The truth is, you vote for one or the other of these two lists every minute of every day." Ouch.

The truth is, even Christian leaders can neglect the care of their own souls in their attempt to care for the souls of others.

Personally, I've known what it means to fail in this area. I crashed through every symptom of soul neglect when working with a team to launch a new church near Boston. Eventually my soul demanded to be heard. I was attempting to do everything in my own strength. Finally I heard the gentle voice of the Shepherd ask, *"Mindy, what part of 'nothing' (in John 15:5) don't you understand?"*

My soul's recovery was a slow one. Thankfully, I had a few soul-guides who led me into a new way of life that keeps me much clearer on my need for authentic connection to God. So my role at Willow Creek now is to highlight our intense conviction about the centrality of the soul and the urgency to find a way of life that keeps the soul healthy. The "how" of soul health is all about cultivating connection and receptivity to God, and that generally takes the form of spiritual practices that open the human soul to God. Woven together, these practices become a way of life that keeps the soul healthy. But living this way does require a fundamental shift, not just a better plan to be more organized or more "spiritual."

Most Christian leaders would agree that certain practices help us "grow." Prayer and Bible study make the top of almost any list. But given the current symptoms, it would appear that more is needed.

In addition to the role of Scripture and self-examination, these four practices are emphasized in our church's efforts towards spiritual formation in leaders.

SPIRITUAL FRIENDSHIP

Spiritual friendship is the intentional pursuit of friends who help you remain open to God. Spiritual friends help each other pay attention to where God is at work in their lives and help each other respond.

Christians often live lonely lives of pretending. Sometimes, they're aware of the pretending; sometimes even they themselves are fooled. Spiritual friendship takes the "everything is together" mask off in very specific, human, in-the-moment ways. It's considered a "practice" because this vulnerability requires a willingness to enter the risky realm of being known as a person in process.

Tobias told me, "I approached friendships exactly as I was advised in seminary: 'Do not befriend anyone in your congregation.'" He had been instructed, "They need to look up to you; they need to see your example, and if you share your struggles, it will undermine your role as their leader."

He continued, "After a painful burnout, it finally dawned on me . . . we're telling ourselves that in order to be effective in ministry, we have to live a lie." Alone.

Admittedly, dangers lurk on the path to authentic relationships. But will we continue to live a lonely lie, or will we navigate these dangers for the hope of life, freedom, and transformation? That hope is well founded. But it will take a concerted effort, and practice, to build a spiritual friendship.

CENTERING PRAYER

In working with groups, I'm often amazed at two things: first, how few enjoy a vibrant experience of prayer; second, how many Christians carry tremendous guilt about their lack of prayer. A double whammy! No wonder we don't like to talk about prayer.

Nonetheless, great healing and fueling power is released from God to us in prayer.

In this form of prayer, there are no more words, no more agendas, no more striving. This is an open, surrendered, peaceful way of resting in the presence of God. Centering prayer is not an absenting of the soul, as in Eastern mysticism, but being very much present with God. It requires practice and patience as your soul learns to become quiet.

Try centering prayer for about twenty minutes once a day for a week. Be prepared for the onslaught of ideas and images that will invade. No matter, you can gently release them and return to the quietness of soul (100 times per minute if your mind is like mine was when I started!). As my friend Lynne told me, "God loves your intent to be attentive, even if your attentiveness wavers with embarrassing frequency."

Over time, you can say, like the psalmist, "But I have stilled and quieted my soul" (Psalm 131:2).

SOLITUDE

This is time alone with God. Why is solitude so potent? Because it frees you for a while from many things that would otherwise drive you. We can be invisibly driven by our egos, our fears, our insecurities, or even other people. Solitude helps us recognize and confront voices other than the Holy Spirit's.

Solitude also protects those unique parts of you that will get lost along the way if not guarded. What is that for you? Do you know what's at stake? Artists might say, "I lose my creativity." Elders say, "I lose my discernment." Leaders may say, "I lose clarity of vision."

Note what Jesus did. After a "run" of demanding ministry commitments, "very early in the morning, while it was still dark, Jesus left the house and went off to a solitary place."

In solitude he regained clarity. It fueled his unflinching resolve. Who today doesn't need clarity amid clamoring voices? Who doesn't need inner resolve to set and keep a direction? We all do. We need times of solitude.

SIMPLICITY

In the wake of the current secular buzz around simplicity, it's important to be clear about what simplicity is and isn't from a biblical perspective. If you were to adopt the view of *RealSimple* magazine, for example, you'd see simplicity as intentional efforts to reduce complexity in your life, to make life more manageable. As nice as that sounds, it's not what we are after.

For a follower of Christ, the enemy of simplicity is not complexity. It's duplicity. Double-mindedness. The apostle Paul hardly led a complexity-free life. But he led a life of deep integrity and focus. That's the simplicity we seek.

Overbooking my schedule is a deeper spiritual issue than merely managing my life's complexities. At its core, it's me being dishonest about who I am and what my limits are. It is an insistence upon self-rule, not upon God's calling.

Simplicity rests on single-mindedness: letting your yes be yes; your no, no. Simplicity is bringing one's whole self into union with God's purposes: every dimension, every thought, and every decision under the direction of God.

I ask individuals to explore areas where they bump into their own duplicity. It may be trying to appear to be more than we are, trying to have more than we can afford, or trying to do more than we really can. Then, to take a courageous step in the direction of simplicity, focusing on God's purposes for you, trusting that your limits are OK.

That's simplicity. That's what leads to soul health.

Mindy Caliguire serves in the area of spiritual formation at Willow Creek Community Church in South Barrington, Illinois. Visit her Web site at *www.soulcare.com*.

Copyright © 2004 by the author or *Christianity Today International/Leadership Journal*. Used by permission.

Daily Bible Readings

EPISODE 1: How Do I See Myself?
Day 1: Psalm 25:15-17
Day 2: Galatians 5:18-20
Day 3: John 16:17-22
Day 4: Ezra 9:4-6
Day 5: Colossians 3
Day 6: Psalm 8

EPISODE 2: Who Am I Really?
Day 1: John 1:1-13
Day 2: 1 John 3:1-10
Day 3: Galatians 2:4, 5; Galatians 5:1
Day 4: Romans 8:28-39
Day 5: 1 Corinthians 5:11-21
Day 6: Psalm 139

EPISODE 3: Who Can I Become?
Day 1: Psalm 52
Day 2: Ephesians 1
Day 3: Ephesians 2
Day 4: 1 Timothy 1:12-20
Day 5: Psalm 138
Day 6: Romans 12

EPISODE 4: How Do I See God?
Day 1: Job 3
Day 2: John 14
Day 3: Matthew 12
Day 4: John 10:11-18
Day 5: Matthew 26:36-39
Day 6: Matthew 11:28-30

EPISODE 5: Is God My Father?
Day 1: Nehemiah 9:16, 17
Day 2: Joel 3:16
Day 3: Deuteronomy 32:1-4
Day 4: 2 Corinthians 1:3-7
Day 5: Psalm 18
Day 6: Matthew 6:9-13

EPISODE 6: What Did Jesus Do for Me?
Day 1: Matthew 27:11-66
Day 2: Luke 24
Day 3: 1 Peter 3:18-22
Day 4: Galatians 4:4-7
Day 5: Romans 6:1-14
Day 6: Hebrews 10:1-10

EPIDSODE 7: Can God Live in Me?
Day 1: Acts 1
Day 2: Acts 2
Day 3: 2 Timothy 1:13, 14
Day 4: Galatians 5:16-26
Day 5: Psalm 51:6-12
Day 6: 1 John 4:12-16

EPISODE 8: Can God Use Me?
Day 1: Ephesians 2:19-22
Day 2: Matthew 28:16-20
Day 3: 1 Corinthians 3:8, 9
Day 4: 1 Corinthians 12
Day 5: 1 Corinthians 14
Day 6: 2 Corinthians 12:7-10

EPISODE 9: What Happens at Home?
Day 1: Joshua 24:15
Day 2: Titus 2:1-8
Day 3: 1 Peter 3:1-7
Day 4: Proverbs 4:3, 4
Day 5: Colossians 3:18-25
Day 6: Ephesians 6:1-4

EPISODE 10: What Happens at Work?
Day 1: 1 Thessalonians 5:12-18
Day 2: Philippians 2
Day 3: Matthew 5:13-16
Day 4: Proverbs 21
Day 5: Judges 6:11-16
Day 6: Proverbs 31

EPISODE 11: What Happens at Church?
Day 1: Matthew 16:13-20
Day 2: Acts 11:19-26
Day 3: Romans 16
Day 4: 1 Timothy 3
Day 5: 1 Peter 5
Day 6: 1 Corinthians 1:1-17

EPISODE 12: What Happens with My Enemies?
Day 1: Matthew 5:1-12
Day 2: Matthew 5:21-26, 38-48
Day 3: Proverbs 16:7
Day 4: Genesis 33
Day 5: 1 Samuel 24
Day 6: Psalm 143

EPISODE 13: How Far Does This Go?
Day 1: 2 Corinthians 3
Day 2: Psalm 18:46-50
Day 3: Acts 8:26-40
Day 4: Acts 10
Day 5: Psalm 96
Day 6: John 3:16, 17